India Ebook's

ONE SHOT FOR IGNOU MPSE-004

SOCIAL & POLITICAL THOUGHT IN MODERN INDIA

M.A. - Political Science
MPS - 2nd Year

JANMEJOY DAS

INDIA EBOOK PRSS

Contents

1. PRE-MODERN SOCIO-RELIGIOUS POLITICAL THOUGHT IN INDIA: THE DIVERSE STRANDS 7

    1.1: One Shot Concepts 7

    1.2: IGNOU Book Exercise - Solved 11

    1.3: IGNOU Past 6 Attempts Question - Solved 11

2. ORIENTALIST DISCOURSE AND COLONIAL MODERNITY 12

    2.1: One Shot Concepts 12

    2.2: IGNOU Book Exercise - Solved 18

    2.3: IGNOU Past 6 Attempts Question - Solved 18

3. SALIENT FEATURES OF MODERN POLITICAL THOUGHT 19

    3.1: One Shot Concepts 19

    3.2: IGNOU Book Exercise - Solved 24

    3.3: IGNOU Past 6 Attempts Question - Solved 25

4. EARLY NATIONALIST RESPONSES: RAMMOHAN ROY, BANKIM CHANDRA CHATTERJEE, DAYANAND SARASWATI AND JYOTIBA PHULE 26

    4.1: One Shot Concepts 26

    4.2: IGNOU Book Exercise - Solved 31

    4.3: IGNOU Past 6 Attempts Question - Solved 31

5. MODERATES AND EXTREMISTS: DADABHAI NAOROJI, MG RANADE AND BG TILAK 35

    5.1: One Shot Concepts 35

    5.2: IGNOU Book Exercise - Solved 39

    5.3: IGNOU Past 6 Attempts Question - Solved 40

6. HINDUISM: SWAMI VIVEKANANDA AND SRI AUROBINDO GHOSH 41

6.1: One Shot Concepts 41

6.2: IGNOU Book Exercise - Solved 53

6.3: IGNOU Past 6 Attempts Question - Solved 54

7. HINDUTVA: V. D. SAVARKAR AND M. S. GOLWALKAR55

7.1: One Shot Concepts 55

7.2: IGNOU Book Exercise - Solved 65

7.3: IGNOU Past 6 Attempts Question - Solved 67

8. MUSLIM THOUGHT: SIR SYED AHMED KHAN, MOHAMMED IQBAL, MAULANA MAUDOODI AND MOHAMMED ALI JINNAH68

8.1: One Shot Concepts 68

8.2: IGNOU Book Exercise - Solved 74

8.3: IGNOU Past 6 Attempts Question - Solved 76

9. NATION & IDENTITY CONCERNS: EV RAMASWAMY NAICKER, NAZRUL ISLAM, PANDITA RAMABAI, JAIPAL SINGH, KHAN SINGH77

9.1: One Shot Concepts 77

9.2: IGNOU Book Exercise - Solved 84

9.3: IGNOU Past 6 Attempts Question - Solved 84

10. M. K. GANDHI 85

10.1: One Shot Concepts 85

10.2: IGNOU Book Exercise - Solved 96

10.3: IGNOU Past 6 Attempts Question - Solved 98

11. JAWAHARLAL NEHRU 99

11.1: One Shot Concepts 99

11.2: IGNOU Book Exercise - Solved 106

11.3: IGNOU Past 6 Attempts Question - Solved ... 107

12. B. R. AMBEDKAR 108

12.1: One Shot Concepts 108

12.2: IGNOU Book Exercise - Solved...................... 110

12.3: IGNOU Past 6 Attempts Question - Solved ... 117

13. RABINDRANATH TAGORE 118

13.1: One Shot Concepts 118

13.2: IGNOU Book Exercise - Solved...................... 122

13.3: IGNOU Past 6 Attempts Question - Solved ... 122

14. COMMUNIST THOUGHT: M N ROY AND E M S NAMBOODIRIPAD
.... 123

14.1: One Shot Concepts 123

14.2: IGNOU Book Exercise - Solved...................... 127

14.3: IGNOU Past 6 Attempts Question - Solved ... 130

15. SOCIALIST THOUGHT: RAMMANOHAR LOHIA AND JAYAPRAKASH
NARAYAN... 131

14.1: One Shot Concepts 131

14.2: IGNOU Book Exercise - Solved...................... 135

14.3: IGNOU Past 6 Attempts Question - Solved ... 136

1. PRE-MODERN SOCIO-RELIGIOUS POLITICAL THOUGHT IN INDIA: THE DIVERSE STRANDS

Introduction
State and Sovereignty in Ancient India
State and Sovereignty in Medieval India
Religion and Polity

1.1: One Shot Concepts

INTRODUCTION

To understand modern Indian political thought, it is essential to have a broad view of the historical processes through which the modern polity has emerged. We have civilisation which is comparable with the Greek civilisation and as Plato and Aristotle are considered as the pioneers of western political tradition, so are our ancient and medicval texts on statecraft.

Whether it is tlie concept of monarchy, republicanism, council of ministers, welfare state, diplomacy, espionage system or any other political concept/institution which is known in modern political parlance, all these have references in our early political traditions. State, society and governance are interlinked to each other. If we look at our past we will find that there was a time when people used to live in small groups based on kinship ties and there was no need felt for all authority to control people's life.

But with the growth of population and clashes between groups of people, the need was felt for an authority who would provide the required protection to his people and whose order would be obeyed by all. With the coming of groups of people together, society came into existence which was followed by the emergence of state and the art of governance.

STATE AND SOVEREIGNTY IN ANCIENT INDIA

IGNOU Book Q.1

The Vedic period represented the lineage system but later on growing stratification in society indicated the tendency towards state formation. With the formation of state the issue of governance of the state became a major concern of the society. In the Shanti Parva of the Mahabharata we find the reference to Matsyanyaya, a condition in which small fishes become prey to big fishes. This analogy was given to explain the anarchic condition in a society where no authority exists. To avoid this type of crisis, people collectively agreed to have a set of laws and to appeal to the god for a king who will maintain law and order in society. It is also argued that without appealing to any divine agency people on their own selected a person on whom the authority was vested to protect human society.

We find references to both Divine Origin of Kingship as well as Social Contract Theory of Kingship. Though theological and metaphysical environment had a strong influence in shaping the ancient Indian thinking, various studies on ancient Indian polity suggest the emergence of polity as an independent domain. Whether it was a Divine Origin of Kingship or Social Contract, we find monarchy as the dominant form of government in the early Indian polity. The seven constituents of the state as prescribed in the Shanti Parva of the Mahabharata are as follows:

Swamin or the sovereign - Swamin or the king is considered as the head of this structure.

Amatya or the officials - Next to him is the Amatya or the council of ministers through which the king governs the state.

Janapada or the territory - Janapada means territory having agricultural land, mines, forests, etc.

Durga or the fort - Durga or fort suggests the fortification of the capital.

Kosa or the treasury - Kosa or treasury, the place where collected revenues are kept.

Danda or the Army - Danda refers to the power of law and of authority.

Mitra or the Allies - Mitra is the friendly state.

<u>Manusmriti</u> strongly advocated for a political authority. **Manu** was of the opinion that in the absence of a political authority, there would be disorder in society. It is the duty of the king to ensure justice in the society and protect the weak. Manu was in favour of social hierarchy and caste system and his notion of justice was based on diverse customs and practices of different castes. He suggested that though the king derived his authority from god, in practice he should be guided by the brahmanas.

In terms of early Indian political thought, **Arthasastra** by *Kautilya* gives a more detailed picture of statecraft. On the chapters dealing with the king and his family, Arthasastra tells us as to how a king should control his senses and discharge his duties, how a king should protect himself from any threat on his life and the importance of selection of right counsellors and priests.

STATE AND SOVEREIGNTY IN MEDIEVAL INDIA
IGNOU Book Q.2

Coming of **Islam** in India and the establishment of the Muslim political authority marked the abeginning of a distinct phase in the Indian political thought. Islamic political thought is centred around the teaching of Muhammad and the belief in the universality of the law of the Koran. In contrast to the Vedantic philosophy, the Muslims consider Koran as the only and final authority.

In Islamic thought the Shariat based on the Koran is considered as the final authority and the purpose of the state is to

serve the Shariat. In matters of governance, the Muslim elite were influenced by political ideas in Islam. Based on two authoritative texts written during the Muslim rule in India- Fatwa-i-Jahandari and Ain-i-Akbari denling with the nuances of governance- we can formulate our ideas about the dominant trend of the political thought of medieval India.

According to **Al Barani**, "It is the duty of the Sultans before they have made up their minds about an enterprise or policy and published it among the people, to reflect carefully on the likelihood of its success and failure as well as its effects on their position, on the religion and the state, and on the army." In Barani's opinion the king should devote himself to governance of his state in such a way that helps him in reaching nearer to God. Welfare of the religion and the state should be the ideal of a good state. A king should be guided by wise men. Bureaucracy is required to run the administration and Barani is an advocate of blue blood aristocracy.

Implementation of law and obedience to law should be the primary concern of a king. Barani refers to four sources of law: a) the *Koran* b) the *Hadish* (traditions of prophet) c) the *Ijma* (opinions and rulings of the majority of Muslim theologians and d) *Qiyas* (speculative method of deduction).

Akbar through the <u>abolition</u> of **jizya** collected from the non-Muslims or a ban on cow slaughter reflected the spirit of new political theory articulated in Ain-i-Akbari. Abul Fazl was a believer in strong centralised monarchical government and for better governance he advocated the distribution of works among various departments. It was with the help of a highly centralised bureaucracy that the Mughal sovereign ruled over the empire.

RELIGION AND POLITY

IGNOU Book Q.3

Discussion on the ***pre-modern Indian political thought*** will remain incomplete if we do not take into account the relationship between religion and polity. Let us begin with the views shared by Gandhi and Maulana Azad regarding religion and politics. *Gandhi* said that those who talk about the separation of religion and politics do not know what religion is. ***Maulana Azad*** wrote, that 'There will be nothing left with us if we separate politics from religion'.

The history of India shows that ours is a unique civilisation which has, over the years, accommodated various religious traditions. In every religion, whether it is Hinduism, Buddhism, Jainism, Islam, Sikhism or Christianity, with the evolution of society and new developments, various sects emerged having differences in expressing their loyalty to the almighty. However these differences were not meant for establishing one's superiority over the other.

Each religion talks about moral values and one's duty towards the other and the society at large. References to the virtues of honesty, humility, selflessness, compassion for the poor, etc. are scattered in the teachings of various religious orders.

Nowhere the distinction has been made among subjects along religious lines although there might have been individual rulers who deviated from this principle. Those deviations should be considered as aberrations rather than the guiding principles of kingship, Here it would be pertinent to refer to ***Dr. S. Radhakrishnan*** who said that 'the religious impartiality of the Indian State is not to be confused with secularism or atheism.

Secularism as here defined is in accordance with the ancient religious tradition of India. Similarly when Islam came to India there might have been attempts by a few to make Islam, state religion but we find that the same period witnessed the growth of Sufism or Akbar's Tauhid-i-Ilahi (called Din-i-Ilahi) which focused on universalism. The same period is important for the growth of Bhakti movement.

1.2: IGNOU Book Exercise – Solved

1. Explain the major features of political ideas in Ancient India.
Answer by India Ebook: Read the 1 Shot Concept Above.

2. Discuss the important ideas regarding sovereign authority during the Medieval period.
Answer by India Ebook: Read the 1 Shot Concept Above.

3. In what way has religion influenced the polity in pre-modern India?
Answer by India Ebook: Read the 1 Shot Concept Above.

1.3: IGNOU Past 6 Attempts Question – Solved

Dec 2021: Write an essay on the distinctive features of pre-modern political thought.
Answer by India Ebook: Almost same as Q.3 of Above.

June 2021: Describe the nature of State and Sovereignty in Medieval India.
Answer by India Ebook: Same as Q.2 of Above.

June 2020: Describe the major features of Political Thought in Ancient India.
Answer by India Ebook: Same as Q.1 of Above.

June 2019: Write an essay on the nature of state and sovereignty in medieval India.
Answer by India Ebook: Same as Q.2 of Above.

2. ORIENTALIST DISCOURSE AND COLONIAL MODERNITY

Introduction

Different Strands of Recent Scholarship

- The Neo-Gandhian Critique
- The Subaltern Studies School
- The Anthropological Studies in the U.S.
- Edward Said's Orientalism

Nationalism and Colonial Modernity

- Nationalism as "Difference"
- Anxieties about the Nation's Women
- Cultural Split and Liberal Ideas
- A Different Sequence and Different Modernity

Nationalism, History and Colonial Knowledge

- Construction of India in the 19th Century
- Nationalist Imagination and Indian History
- Orientalism and the Colony's Self Knowledge

2.1: One Shot Concepts

INTRODUCTION

In the last few decades, particularly since the 1980s, this field has given rise to a whole new body of work and serious, often very sharp debates among scholars. It was during this period that an intense and fresh engagement with the whole question of our colonial modernity came to the fore. What is crucially important about this development in the scholarship on the Indian subcontinent is that it focuses, unlike earlier writings on colonial history, on the politics of knowledge implicated in that history. In a very significant way, it foregrounds the manner in which our knowledge of 'our own' history - and our own selves - is framed by and understood through categories produced by colonial knowledge.

DIFFERENT STRANDS OF RECENT SCHOLARSHIP   IGNOU Book Q.1

There are at least **four (4)** different strands of scholarship that have come together since the 1980s, that have been at the root of this transformation.

➤ The Neo-Gandhian Critique

In the first place, there has been since the early 1980s, the reactivation of an older Gandhian critique of modernity. Central in this strand has been the work of scholars like Ashis Nandy, Veena Das and scholar-activists active in the environment and science movements like Claude Alvares and Vandana Shiva. Much of the critique of this set of scholars has been directed at a critique of science and rationality as the ruling ideological coordinates of modernity, alongside the related notion of development followed by the Nehruvian state. Though not all scholars associated with this strand have an explicitly Gandhian orientation, they broadly extend elements of Gandhi's rejection of modern Western civilisation and its faith in science and reason as the conditions of human freedom.

➤ The Subaltern Studies School

The second strand can be identified in the work of the Subaltern Studies School of Indian Historiography. This school too made its first public appearance on the scene in the early 1980s - although its work began in the late 1970s. This group of historians and some political scientists came from a primarily Left-wing political background and much of their initial work was a continuation of the concerns that they had developed through the impact of Maoist political practice in the 1970s.

➤ The Anthropological Studies in the US

The third strand comes from within the field of area studies from anthropologists like Bernard Cohn, largely situated in the United States. Bernard Cohn's work spans a much longer period starting from the mid-1950s. Ile had been writing on questions relating to colonial knowledge of India and the ways in which this knowledge transformed the very society it claimed to study. His researches also showed how these knowledges constituted political subjectivities in the colonial world.

➤ Edward Said's Orientalism

Finally, there is the work of Palestinian-American scholar, Edward Said that could be said to have made possible the coming together of these different bodies of work. With the publication in the 1978, of Said's highly acclaimed tract Orientalism, different efforts to deal with the continuing legacy of the West in the former colonies as well as in immigrant communities in the West received a major fillip. In this tract, which became vely influential in and around the mid-1980s, Said showed how certain constructions of the East or the 'Orient' have been crucial to Europe's self-image.

NATIONALISM & COLONIAL MODERNITY   IGNOU Book Q.2

Two things started becoming apparent in the course of these explorations. First, that nationalism was not simply one monolithic ideological formation that every modern society must have. The situation was complicated by the fact that societies like India's were inserted into modernity by the agency of colonialism. Second, as a consequence, it was also becoming apparent that nationalism therefore, also involved a formidable and creative intellectual intervention, formulating and defending its main postulates in the battlefield of politics, as Partha Chatterjee put it.

➢ Nationalism as Difference

Let us now turn to some of the features of nationalism and colonial modernity as we know it today from the work of scholars mentioned above. Attaining the nationhood and selfgovernance, the nationalists understood, was the only way to be modern. That was the way the world they discovered, actually was.

Nehru highlights one of the most abiding inner conflicts of Indian, but more generally, of all post-colonial nationalisms. If we remember that Nehru was by far the most radical of modernists among all the nationalists, we can imagine what would have been the situation of other nationalist leaders. In fact this is an anxiety that is evident among the intellectual elite of Indian society long before the formal appearance of nationalism towards the end of the 19th century.

➢ Anxieties About the Nation's Women

The concern with women is evident in both, Nandy's exploration of Sati and Chakravarty's explorations of domesticity. It is the 'Women's Question' therefore, argues Partha Chatterjee, that becomes the site for a major nationalist intervention. Chatterjee explores what he calls the nationalist resolution of the women's question to suggest that the way in which nationalism sought to mark out its difference was by demarcating a sphere of inner sovereignty.

Nationalism starts its journey by demarcating an 'inner' and an 'outer' sphere and declaring itself sovereign in the inner; cultural sphere. In the outer sphere its subjugation is a given fact, but in the inner domain of culture it claims complete sovereignty. It refuses to make the question of women a matter of negotiation with the colonial state. On the other hand, it does not simply rest content with the old status of women. It rather embarks on a project of creating a 'new woman', educated, active in public life and at the same time fully aware of her domestic, womanly duties.

> ### Cultural Split and Liberal Ideas IGNOU Book Q.3

Sudipta Kaviraj introduces three more interesting aspects in his delineation of the features of colonial modernity. *First*, he argues, modern colonial education introduced a split in the Indian cultural life, by bringing into being two "rather exclusive spheres of English and vernacular discourse." The concerns that animated these different spheres were very different. While the English-speaking world was more concerned with ideas of individual liberty, those working in the vernacular world were far less concerned with democracy as a form of government. The vernacular nationalist intelligentsia was more concerned with the problem of "collective freedom of the Indian people from British rule" rather than with that of individual freedom.

Indian nationalist elite encountered the great liberal ideas of equality, freedom and autonomy in a context of subjugation and were therefore, more immediately concerned with issues of national sovereignty. They, therefore, chose to transfer these ideas into their own concerns. Here, we see the second feature: Liberal ideas, Kaviraj contends, did have 'a deep and profound influence in Indian political argument" but this influence was not in terms of implanting liberal ideas but nationalist ones. This is not a minor or trivial difference but in a sense crucial, for as Kaviraj points out, the idea of equality between nations or societies can be completely blind to the idea of internal equality within the national community. Hence, even somebody like Gandhi could easily justify the caste system while claiming national equality & freedom from the British

> ### A Different Sequence and Different Modernity

This second feature, according to Kaviraj, is also linked to a third: Modernity in India followed a very different sequence from that in the West. Modernity is a historical constellation, Kaviraj argues, that comprises three distinct processes: capitalist industrial production, political institutions of liberal democracy and the emergence of a society where old community bonds have been largely dissolved and the process of individuation has taken place. This means that in the place of old forms of belonging, there have emerged new interest-based associations.

This is what is called in political theory, 'the space of civil society'. In the historical trajectory of the West, democracy emerged after the other two processes had developed to a high degree. Initial disciplining of the working class, for instance, took place in a context where there was no possibility of democratic resistance. In fact, democratic aspirations were, at least partly, a consequence of the process of capitalist industrialisation. In India, on the other hand, democracy and parliamentary institutions preceded the other two processes. Kaviraj links this different sequence to a kind of populist politics that comes to dominate the political scene in India and many post-colonial countries.

NATIONALISM, HISTORY AND COLONIAL KNOWLEDGE

Nationalism, assuming that there was one single entity called nationalism - and that was Indian nationalism. As it happens, there was neither a single nationalism, nor for that matter, a single Indian nationalism. We know, for example, that the Indian National Congress exposed one kind of Indian nationalism that we may call "secular-nationalism'.

We also know that the Muslim League espoused, at least from around 1940 onwards, a Pakistani nationalism. This is often referred to as the 'two-nation theory'. This was also propounded by someone like Vinayak Damodar Savarkar who stood for an explicitly Hindu-Indian nationalism. We also know for instance, that there was during the nationalist period a Bengali nationalism, an Assamese nationalism, a Malayali nationalism and such other nationalisms. India represents a **'unity in diversity'**. And yet, what if you are told that before the nineteenth century, nobody exactly knew the physical stretch of this landmass & that our ancestors had no idea of how many communities & religions existed in this land. Nor did they have any idea of how many people there were in each community.

> **Construction of India in the 19th Century**   IGNOU Book Q.4

Talte for instance the fact that the first tentative maps of 'India' - the name for India too did not exist at that time - were drawn up by James Rennell, a colonial official in Bengal, between 1782 and 1788. It was only by 1818 that, with the East India Company's annexation of large parts of the subcontinent, that an idea of the geographical stretch of the land began to emerge. It was only in the 19th century that the idea of a geographical entity called 'India' was consolidated.

It was also in the 19th century that the first censuses of India were done and only in 1881 that the first comprehensive census took place. It was then that the idea of the different communities that inhabited the land became available, as also their numbers. As there were no clear-cut notions of community, the British defined them in their own ways for purposes of classification. Large categories such as 'Hindu' and 'Muslim', as well as those of caste (in which they fitted thousands of jntis) were in a sense, colonial constructs, devised primarily for the purpose of census enumerations.

One of the major facts that emerges then from the discussion of colonial governmental practices is that our very idea of India, its geographical boundaries, its population and its cultural composition etc are all formed by the knowledge produced by the colonial state. What is most important is that all subsequent politics, including nationalist politics, was shaped by this knowledge. In the initial phases of the nationalist movement, it was not really clear what nationalism was all about.

➤ **Nationalist Imagination and Indian History**

For the very idea of nationhood required that the new political commmunity lay claim to an ancient history. For the large part of the 19th century therefore, we see early nationalists vigorously at work to invent a history of India. As Kaviraj puts, in this period, particularly in Bengal, "history breaks out everywhere". Important thinkers like Bankimchandra Chattopadhyay proclaim, "we must have a history". Bankim in fact, puts it more vehemently that "Even when they go hunting for birds, sahebs [i.e. Britishers] write its history, but also, Bengalis have no history." Notice that even at this stage, Bankim was only thinking of Bengal and Bengali as his nation.

➤ **Orientalism and the Colony's Self-knowledge**   IGNOU Book Q.5

It is well known that academic knowledge about India - its history - was produced by the efforts of the great Orientalist scholars of the late 18th and 19th centuries. The founding of the Asiatic Society of Bengal in 1784, by British Orientalists like William Jones, can be considered as a milestone in this enterprise. O. P. Kejariwal's The Asiatic Society of

Bengal and the Discovery of India's Past for instance documents the work of this pioneering institution in the excavation of India's past.

You might be surpfised to know, as Kejariwal was when he started looking at the work of the Asiatic Society, that till as late as 1834, the names of ancient emperors like Samudragupta and Chandragupta Maurya were not known to anybody.

Like other nations, it is the work of a collective imagination that was at work from the second half of the 19th century onwards, which deftly appropriated the work done by Orientalist scholars, in order - to produce the narrative of a great and ancient civilisation. This was the nationalist imagination that retrospectively produced a History of the Nation, in which all the separate histories of the different entities that today form a part of the landmass called India, became reconfigured as the History of India. Now, the fact that "we did not have a history" before the 19th century should not be understood to mean that 'we' did not have any sense or relationship with the past. Nationalists of the 19th and early 20th centuries routinely saw this as a sign of ourm backwardness, of a - 'lack' that showed that we were not modern.

2.2: IGNOU Book Exercise - Solved

1. Discuss different strands of thought among scholars on the question of colonial modernity.
Answer by India Ebook: Read the 1 Shot Concept Above.

2. Explain Nationalism's concern with orientalism and colonial discourse.
Answer by India Ebook: Read the 1 Shot Concept Above.

3. Discuss Nationalism and its features with reference to liberal ideas.
Answer by India Ebook: Read the 1 Shot Concept Above.

4. Critically examine the Construction of India in the 19th Century.
Answer by India Ebook: Read the 1 Shot Concept Above.

5. Discuss Orientalism and the colony's self-knowledge.
Answer by India Ebook: Read the 1 Shot Concept Above.

2.3: IGNOU Past 6 Attempts Question - Solved

Dec 2020: Explain the different strands of Nationalism in India.
Answer by India Ebook: Almost same as Q.2 of Above.

3. SALIENT FEATURES OF MODERN POLITICAL THOUGHT

Introduction

Two Phases of Modern Indian Thought

Social Reform and the "Hindu Renaissance"

➢ Two Intellectual Moves of Reformers

➢ Modes of Reformist Thought

The Arrival of Nationalism

➢ The 'Inner' and 'Outer' Domains

➢ Concerns of Nationalists

The Trajectory of Muslim Thought

➢ The Specificity of Muslim History and Thought

➢ The Reform Initiative

➢ The Anti-Imperialist Currents

The Revolt of the Lower Orders

3.1: One Shot Concepts

INTRODUCTION

This unit deals with the salient features of modern Indian political thought. This is not an easy exercise as there is no single body of thought that we call call 'Indian'. Nor is there a continuity of concerns across time - say between the early 19th century and the late 19th century. Taking a synoptic view therefore necessarily reduces the complexities and does not do full justice to minority or subordinate voices, relegating them further to the margins. You will do well to bear in mind that most of the modern Indian political and social thought is marked by the experience of the colonial encounter. It was within this universe that most of our thinkers, hailing from different communities and social groups, embarked on their intellectual-political journey.

TWO PHASES OF MODERN INDIAN THOUGHT IGNOU Book Q.1

We call broadly divide modern Indian thought into two phases. The first phase was that of what has often been referred to as the phase of 'Social Reform'. Thinkers of this phase, as we shall see, were more concerned with the internal regeneration of indigenous society and because its first effervescence occurred in Bengal, it was often referred to as the 'Bengal Renaissance'. Nationalist historians of course, even started referring to it as the Indian Renaissance. The second phase, more complex and textured in many ways, is the phase that we can designate as the nationalist phase.

Before we go into the specific features of the thinkers of the two broad periods that we have outlined, it is necessary to make a few clarifications. Though most scholars have tended to see these as two distinct phases or periods, this way of looking at the history of modern Indian political thought can be quite problematic. These periodisations can only be very broad and tentative ones, made for the purpose of convenience of study; on no account should they be rendered into fixed and hermetically sealed periods.

In fact, we can more productively see them as two broad currents which do not necessarily follow one after the other. As we shall see, there are many social reform concerns that take on a different form and continue into the nationalist phase. In fact, the nationalist phase itself reveals two very distinct tendencies in this respect.

On the one hand, there is the dominant or hegemonic nationalism, represented in the main by the Indian National Congress, where the social reform agenda is abandoned in a significant way; on the other there are other contending narratives that insist on privileging the reform agenda much to the discomfort of the nationalists.

SOCIAL REFORM AND THE "HINDU RENAISSANCE'

IGNOU Book Q.2

There was a veritable explosion of intellectual activity throughout the 19th century, particularly in Bengal and Western India. In Bengal there was the Young Bengal movement, and publicists, thinkers and social reformers like Raja Rammohan Roy, Iswarchandra Vidyasagar, Keshub Chandra Sen, Michael Madhusudan Dutta, Surendranath Banerjee, Swami Vivekananda and such other personalities who embodied this effervescence.

In Western India there were reformers like Bal Shastri Jambhekar, Jotirao Govindrao Phule, Ramakrishna Gopal Bhandarkar, Gopal Ganesh Agarkar and Swami Dayanand Saraswati (whose activity was mainly in North India), such other luminaries who directly addressed the question of internal regeneration of Indian society.

They launched the nzost vigorous critique of their own society, with the aim of bringing it out of its backwardness. As Rammohan Roy put it, it was the "thick clouds of superstition" that "hung all over the land" (i.e. Bengal), that worried him most. Idolatory and priestcraft were often held responsible by thinkers like Dayanand Saraswati, for the destruction of the yearning for knowledge. He believed that it was institutions such as these that had made Hindus fatalist and inert. The issues that dominated the concerns of the social reformers were primarily related to the status of women in Indian society. Sati, widow remarriage and the education of women were central issues raised by the reformers. To this end, they re-interpreted tradition, often offered ruthless critiques of traditional practices and even lobbied support with the colonial government for enacting suitable legislations for banning some of the more obnoxious practices like Sati.

➢ Two Intellectual Moves of Reformers

There are two distinct moves made by the reformers that we must bear in mind. First, their critiques drew very explicitly from the exposure to Western liberal ideas. To many of them Birtish power was the living proof of the validity and 'invincibility' of those ideas. They were therefore, open admirers of British rule. For instance, as Bal Shastri Jambhekar saw it, a mere sixty or seventy years of British rule over Bengal had transformed it beyond recognition.

➢ Modes of Reformist Thought

Bhikhu Parekh has suggested that the arguments of these Hindu reformers relied on one or more of the following four modes of arguments derived from tradition but deployed with a distinct newness to meet the demands of changing times. First, they appealed to scriptures that seemed to them to be more hospitable to their concerns. Vidyasagar for instance relied on the Parasharasmriti, while Rammohan Roy invoked the Upanishads.

Second, they invoked what they called sadharand/zarnza, which they interpreted to mean the universal principles of morality. Third, they appealed to the idea of a yugadharnza, or the principle that accord with the needs of the prevailing yuga or epoch. Fourthly, they invoked the idea of loksangraha, and "argued that the practice in question had such grave consequences that unless eradicated, it would destroy the cohesion and viability of the Hindu social order." As instances, he mentions that Vidyasagar argued that unmarried widows were turning to prostitution or corrupting their families; K.C. sen contended that child marriages were endangering the survival of the Hindu jati; Dayananda Saraswati believed that image worship was leading to internal sectarian quarrels.

THE ARRIVAL OF NATIONALISM

Nationalism could be said to have made its appearance in the last part of the 19th century. In this phase, the concerns and approach of the thinkers change in a very significant way. Here there is a strong concern with the 'freedom of the nation' and an almost irreconcilable hostility towards colonial rule. Unlike the social reformers before them, they placed no trust on the institutions of the colonial state for effecting any reform. On the contrary, they displayed a positive opposition to what they now considered the 'interference' by the colonial state in the 'internal matters' of the nation. Alongside this, there is a parallel move towards privileging of the political struggle over social reforms.

> ➤ **Concerns of the Nationalists**   IGNOU Book Q.3

At this stage, it is necessary to point out that it will be wrong to see the divisions between different strands as those between 'progressives' and 'conservatives' or 'modernists' and 'traditionalists'. For, as many scholars have pointed out, even the nationalists who rejected the standpoint of the reformers, were working for a thoroughly modernist agenda. Their valorisation of Hindu tradition was not a valorisation of existing practices of *Hindu religion*. In fact, they all wanted, much like the reformers, a modern and reorganised Hindu society that would become the centre-piece of the emerging nation. Being 'Hindu' to them was the sign of national identity rather than a religious one.

This concern with 'Hinduness' as a marker of national, rather than religious identity was very much there not only in the case of Congress nationalists but also of **Vinayak Damodar Savarkar**, the author of the ideology of **Hindutva**. In fact, Savarkar greatly valued the work done by Ambedkar and unlike Gandhi who was suspicious of his motives, he associated him with his Hindu Mahasabha functions. What is even more interesting is that *Savarkar's critique* of Gandhi was precisely because of Gandhi's wholesale rejection of modern civilisation, science and technology. In a sense, like Nehru the secular-nationalist, Savarkar's complaint with Gandhi related to his 'irrationality' and 'backward-looking' ideas.

This is precisely the conundrum of the nationalist phase that has eluded many scholars and historians. For, it is the proclaimed anti-modernist and *sanatani Hindu Gandhi* who stood steadfastly for **Hindu-Muslim unity** as the precondition of India's freedom, while the modernist and secular leaders like Madan Mohan Malaviya, Purushottamdas Tandon and Ganesh Shankar Vidyarthi often seemed to be speaking a language of Hindu nationalism. It was Gandhi who made the *Khilafat-Non*

Cooperation movement collaboration of Hindus and Muslims possible.
It is true that Gandhi's insistence on a Hindu sanatnni identity could not eventually convince either the Muslims or the Dalit/Lower caste leaders about his sincerity in safeguarding their interests.

THE TRAJECTORY OF MUSLIM THOUGHT   IGNOU Book Q.4

We have traced the broad contours of 19th and 20th century thought as it emerged from within Hindu society. The history of Muslim society in India is still steeped in a sea of ignorance and misconceptions and a lot more work needs to be done to unearth the different kinds of trends of thought that emerged from within it.

With regard to Muslim society in India, we might need to steer clear of two diametrically opposed viewpoints. One, represented by Hindu nationalists, which sees Muslims as an alien body continuously at odds with and insulated from local society and culture, and the other represented by the secular-nationalists who see merely a syncretic culture that expressed the combined elements of Islamic and Hindu culture. We need to see the process by which what was once and elite Perso-lslarnic culture of the ashrafs (the gentry or the nobility), gradually enters into a dialogue with the local traditions of learning, of the arts and music etc.

> ## The Specificity of Muslim History and Thought

The advent of British rule meant a more immediate loss of political power for the ruling Muslim elite, especially in North India and Bengal. And this contest with British power continued through the century from the *Battle of Plassey* (1757) to the *Great Revolt* – the so-called 'Mutiny' - of **1857**, which saw a massive participation of **Muslims** as a whole and, not merely of the elite.

As a consequence, in the immediate period following the institution of the power of the British, the relationship between the erstwhile ruling elite and the colonial rulers came to be marked by deep hostility and antagonism, One of the consequences of this hostility was a certain inwardness that came to define Muslim attitude towards the modern. By and large, they seemed to stay away from English education and ideas and institutions associated with British power.

However, after the *revolt of 1857*, Western education was discontinued and could only be restarted in 1864. Nonetheless, the fact that such an institution was established indicates a certain openness towards Western knowledge, despite the overall experience of hostility vis-his the British. Mujeeb Ashraf, in fact, claims that Delhi college became one of the models for institutions like Jamia Millia Islamia in the later period. Delhi College produced important 19th century reformers and writers like Zakaullah, Muhammad Husain Azad and Nazir Ahmad Nazir.

➢ The Reform Initiative

The crucial turning point in this respect, however, is the emergence of Sir Syed Ahmad Khan (1817-99) who is known to be the harbinger of liberalism and modernity in Muslim society. He opposed the Great Revolt as he believed that not only had British rule come to stay but also that there was much to be gained by imbibing modern ideas from its contact. It is well known that in order to propagate modern scientific knowledge, he established his Mahommedan Anglo-Oriental College, which in due course, became the Aligarh Muslim University.

➢ The Anti-imperialist Currents

The Aligarh school came under fierce attack from the more theologically inclined Muslims - the learned Ulama. The conflict between the Aligarh school and the Ulama has often been seen as the conflict between the 'modernisers' and the 'traditionalists' but this is in some sense an over simplification. The Ulama's main problem with Syed Ahmad seems to have been with what they considered his eulogisation of the British - his Angreziyat or Englishness. There was here something parallel to what we witnessed in the case of the nationalists departure from the social reformers, insofar as the Ulama saw his Angreziyat as being too collaborationist. It is interesting therefore that his most strident critics were also those who were more clearly anti-imperialist and sought to ally with the nationalist movement for liberation from the British rule.

3.2: IGNOU Book Exercise – Solved

1. Discuss the phases of modern Indian Thought.

Answer by India Ebook: Read the 1 Shot Concept Above.

2. Explain the relevance of Social Reform Movement in India.

Answer by India Ebook: Read the 1 Shot Concept Above.

3. Explain the different concerns of Nationalism in India.

Answer by India Ebook: Read the 1 Shot Concept Above.

4. Discuss various aspects of Muslim Thought in India.

Answer by India Ebook: Read the 1 Shot Concept Above.

5. Explain the role of the Political Leadership to reform Indian Society led by lower order.

Answer by India Ebook: The important point that needs to be registered here in relation to the work and thought of lower caste leaders like Jotirao Phule, EVR Ramaswamy Naicker - also known as Periyar - and B.R. Ambedkar is that it differed from the trends identified in the case of both Hindu and Muslim thought in two crucial ways. Firstly, at no point did these thinkers give up the social reform agenda and in fact their consistent critique of nationalism remained linked to this question.

Secondly, they did not suffer from the deep ambivalence with regard to the West that marked the thought of reformers and nationalists alike in the case of the Hindu thinkers or of Shibli Numani, Muhsin-ul-Mulk and Iqbal in the case of the Muslims.

It is important to note in this context, that to most leaders of the lower castes, particularly the Dalits, the notion of a putative Hindu community simply did not carry any positive significance. To them, the memories of past and continuing humiliation and degradation through practices like untouchability and violent exclusion from society as such, constituted their over-riding experience that framed all their responses. In their perception, therefore, there was something insincere in the efforts of even the reformers who merely wanted the assimilation of lower castes into mainstream Hindu society without disturbing the power structure in anyway.

Social reform not in the vague sense of 'uplift' of the untouchables that Gandhi was seeking to do, without of course disturbing the power of the upper caste elite - but in the more radical sense given to it by Phule. These thinkers and leaders also realised that if the British were to leave without the question of power being settled, they would be yoked into slavery once again. It is from this fear that the main plank of Ambedkar's and Periyar's political life emerged: the vexed question of 'safeguards' or 'communal proportional representation' as it was also called. The radical lower caste leaders realised that independence would come, sooner or later; thus it was necessary to stake a claim for power by bargaining hard on the question of safeguards, while the British were still here. It is this battle that Ambedkar was forced to partially lose thanks to Gandhi's emotional blackmail - his notorious fast-unto-death and the eventual **Poona Pact.**

3.3: IGNOU Past 6 Attempts Question – Solved

June 2020: Explain the relevaence of Social Reform Movements in India.

Answer by India Ebook: Almost same as Q.2 of Above.

Dec 2018: Explain the major concerns of Nationalism in India.

Answer by India Ebook: Almost same as Q.3 of Above.

Dec 2018: Discuss the emergence of Social reform movement in early colonial India.

Answer by India Ebook: Almost same as Q.2 of Above.

4. EARLY NATIONALIST RESPONSES: RAMMOHAN ROY, BANKIM CHANDRA CHATTERJEE, DAYANAND SARASWATI AND JYOTIBA PHULE

Introduction
Early, Nationalist Response
Thoughts of Rammohan Roy
Bankim's Ideas in Shaping Nationalism
Religio-Political Ideas of Dayanand Saraswati
Jyotiba Phule: A Social Revolutionary
Nationalist Response: A Critical Appraisal

4.1: One Shot Concepts

INTRODUCTION

There arc *two* different phases of Indian nationalism. The **first** one continues till the formation of the Indian National Congress in 1885 whereas nationalism, in its **second phase**, was articulated through popular mobilisation around various kinds of anti-imperial ideologies. Of all the competing ideologies, Gandhian 'non violence' was perhaps the most popular ideology in organising anti-imperial movements in India. Unlike the second phase when the national intervention was primarily political, viz., the capture of state power, the first phase was largely dominated by the zeal of reform that appeared to have brought together various individuals wilh more or less same ideological agenda.

EARLY NATIONALIST RESPONSE   IGNOU Book Q.1

The *first* formidable influence was definitely the Enlightenment philosophy that significantly influenced the famous 1832 Macaulay's minutes. Seeking to organise Indian society in a typical Western mould, Macaulay argued for an introduction of English education and British jurisprudence for their role in radically altering the feudal basis of Indian society. What was implicit in his views was the assumption that the liberal values of the British variety would definitely contribute to the required social transformation in India. So, the arrival of the British in India was a boon in disguise. Not only did colonialism introduce Indians to Western liberalism but it also exposed them to the socially and politically progressive ideas of Bentham, Mill, Carlyle and Coleridge, which drew attention to a qualitatively different mode of thinking on issues of contemporary relevance.

The *second* equally important influence was the ideas of **German philosophers**, Selielling, Fichte, Kant ahd Herder. These ideas gained ground as the intellectual challenge against the British rule acquired momentum. In fact, there are <u>clear traces</u> of *German ideas in Bankim's writings*. Unlike **Ram Mohan Roy** whose historical mission was to combat the social evils in the form of inhuman customs, including the sattee, Bankim sought to champion the goal of freedom by drawing upon the German philosophy and Hindu past.

The *third* significant influence in the early phase of <u>Indian nationalism</u> was the **French revolution** and its message for Liberty, Equality and Fraternity. Ram Mohan was swayed by the ideas that inspired the French revolution. In his writings and deeds, Roy launched a vigorous attack on the archaic social mores dividing India along caste and religious cleavages.

The *final* source is of course the traditional Indian thought that was interpreted in the context of colonial rule. Not only were there writings of Williarn Jones and Max Muller on India's rich cultural traditions, there were cotitributions from the renaissance thinkers, including Vivekananda, that provided the basis for redefining India's past glossing largely the phase of Muslim rule in India. Inspired by the message of Bhagvad Gita, the renaissance thinkers supported the philosophy of action in the service of the motherland.

THOUGHTS OF RAMMOHAN ROY

Rammohan Roy was a social thinker par excellence. His role in doing away with sattee among the orthodox Brahmins was historical. By founding *Brahma Samaj*, Roy sought to articulate his belief in the Islamic notion of 'one god'. Altlzough he despised colonialism, he appeared to have endorsed the British rule presumably because of its historical role in combating the prevalent feudal forces. Not only was the British rule superior, at least, culturally than the erstwhile feudal rulers, it would also contribute to a different India by injecting the values it represented. His admiration for the British rule was based oil his faith in its role in radically altering traditional mental make-up of the Hindus.

The continued British rule, he further added, would eventually lead to the establishment of democratic institutions as in Great Britain. Like any other liberals, Roy also felt that the uncritical acceptance of British liberal values was probably the best possible means of creating democratic institutions in India. The other area for which the role of Ram Mohan was, decisive was the articulation of demand for the freedom of press. Along with his colleague, Dwarkanath Tagore, he submitted a petition to the Privy Council for the freedom of press, which he justified as essential for democratic functioning of the government.

Rammohan Roy had played a progressive role in a particular historical context. While conceptualising his historical role, Roy appeared to have privileged his experience of British colonialism over its immediate feudal past. By undermining the obvious devastating impact of foreign rule on Indian society, politics and economy, he also clearly supported one system of administration over the other rather consciously simply because of his uncritical faith in British Enlightenment in significantly trunsforming the prevalent Indian mindsets.

BANKIIM'S IDEAS IN SHAPING NATIONALISM   Dec 2018

Bnnkimchandra Chattopadhyay (1838-94) was probably the first systematic expounder in India of the idea of nationalism. His unique contribution lay in conceptualising nationalism in indigenous terms. In opposition to the Muslim rule, Bankim elaborated the idea by drawing upon the **Bhagavad Gita** that was widely translated in Bengali in the 19th century. In his translated version of Gita, what Bankim provided was a reinterpretation in the light of Western knowledge to make the Gita more suitable reading for the Western-educated intelligentsia in the newly emerged context of the nationalist opposition to the British rule. An entirely new Gita emerged reflecting the concerns of those seeking to provide a national alternative to foreign rule.

What was primary in Bankim's thought was his concern for national solidarity for on it depended the growth of the Hindu society. National solidarity is conceivable, as Bankim argued, only when there is a change in one's attitude in the following two ways: *first*, the conviction that what is good for evely Hindu is good for me and my views, beliefs and actions must be consistent with those of other members of the Hindu society. And, *secondly*, one should inculcate a single-minded devotion to the nation and its interests.

RELIGIO-POLITICAL IDEAS OF DAYANAND SARASWATI

While Bankim had a clear political message for the nation that lacked solidarity, **Dayananda** (1825-83) who founded the *Arya Samaj* had concerns similar to those of Rammohan. Primarily a social reformer, the latter believed that the success of the British in subjugating the Hindu society was largely due to its divisive nature and also the failure in realising its strength. If Rammohan drew upon Upanishads, Bankim upon the Gita, Dayanand while articulating his nationalist response, was inspired by Vedas. The other contrasting point that marked Dayananda off from the rest lies in the utter absence of the influence of European culture and thought on him.

Unlike them, Dayananda found the Vedic messages as most appropriate for inspiring the moribund nation, plagued by several 'ills' that could easily be cured. Seeking to construct a strong Hindu society, Dayananda, was strikingly different from other early nationalists in two specific ways: *first*, his response was essentially based on a conceptualisation that is absolutely indigenous in nature presumably because he was not exposed to the Western ideas. Unique in his approach, Dayananda therefore interrogated the processes of history in a language that added a new dimension to the early nationalist response. *Secondly*, his response was also an offshoot of a creative dialogue with the traditional scriptures, especially the Vedas - which appeared to have influenced the later Extremist leadership for its appeal to distinct civilisational characteristics of India. Unlike those who were drawn to Western liberal ideas, Dayananda was probably the only thinker of his generation to have begun a debate on the relative importance of the ancient scriptures in inspiring a nation that was divided on innumerable counts.

JYOTIBA PHULE: A SOCIAL REVOLUTIONARY

Jotirao Phule (1827-9O), like Dayananda, had the dcsire for a form of social organisation that would reflect the merits and aptitudes of the individual, rather than enforcing birth as the basis both for occupation and for religious status. The play, Tritiya Ratna (The Third Eye), which he published in 1855 is a powerfull exposition of his ideology. The play is about the exploitation of an ignorant and superstitious peasant couple by a cunning Brahmin priest and their subsequent enlightenment by a Christian missionary. Three important points stand out in this play.

First, critical of Brahmin domination, he made a wider point concerning the oppressive nature of Hindu religion that, in its present form, imposed an ideological hegemony on the Shudras and by suggesting several purifying rituals, it also contributed to material impoverishment of the untouchables.

Secondly, by underlining the role of a Christain missionary who rescued the people from the cluthes of the greedy Brahmin, Phule seemed to have explored the possibility of conversion as probably the only practical device to get-out of the exploiatative Hindu religion.

Thirdly, underlying this story, there remained another major ideological point concerning the importance of education in sustaining the Brahminic hegemony in Hindu society. He was persuaded to believe that access to education, and particularly, literacy in English, conferred vital social resources on the Brahmins as a social group.

NATIONALIST RESPONSE: A CRITICAL APPRAISAL

IGNOU Book Q.3

Another major characteristic of the early nationalist response is the way the nation was conceptualised. By avoiding reference to Muslims, these nationalist thinkers seemed to have clearly identified the constituents of the proposed nation. By drawing on exclusively Hindu traditional tracts like Upanishads or Vedas, the early nationalists identified the sources of inspiration for the nation at its formative phase that clearly set the ideological tone in opposition to Islam and its supportive texts. Their idea of nation had therefore a narrow basis since Muslims hardly figured in the conceptualisation. The explanation probably lies in the historical context characterised by the declining decadent feudal culture, supported by the Muslim rulers on the one hand and the growing acceptance of the values of European modernity on the other. Apart from Bankim who had strong views on the Muslim rule, none of the early nationalist thinkers articulated their opinion on this issue in clear terms. What drove them to embark on a nationalist project was the mission to revamp and revitalise the Hindus who failed to emerge as a solid block due largely to the inherent divisive nature.

Whether it was Dayananda or Bankim, the idea of consolidating the Hindus as a race seemed to have acted in a decisive manner while articulating their response. Given his interest in Persian literature and Islamic culture, Rammohan held different views from Bankim. Since Phule was critical of the dichotomous Hindu society, he argued in a reformist language and reference to Muslims did not appear to be relevant. In his perception, the British rule was providential simply because it provided him with intellectual resources to combat the archaic practices in Hinduism.

4.2: IGNOU Book Exercise – Solved

1. What was the basic argument in the early nationalist response for rejuvenating the moribund Hindu society?

Answer by India Ebook: Read the 1 Shot Concept Above.

2. How do you account for the difference between Rammohan, Bankim and Phule on the one hand and Dayananda on the other?

Answer by India Ebook: Rammohan, Bankim, Dayananda or Phule - was the concern for massive reform in Hindu society that lost its vitality. Given the fractured nature of Hindu society, it would be difficult, if not impossible, they argued, for the nation to strike roots, let alone prosper. Drawn on his liberal values of the British variety, Rammohan welcomed the foreign rule as a significant step towards radically transforming the Hindu society by injecting the basic ideas of Enlightenment.

With an uncritical faith in Gita, Bankim found in **anushilan dharma** an appropriate device to galvanise a moribund nation. While **Dayananda distinguished** himself from the rest by depending exclusively on the Vedas, Phule appeased to have been influenced by Western Enlightenment in articulating his views on reform. There is an implicit assumption in what they wrote attributing the triumph of the British to the divisive nature of Hindu society.

While Bankim endorsed Western superiority in the material domain and hence their success, he however drew on the spiritual resources of the Hindus in instilling a sense of identity. Interestingly, this was the running thread in the writings of Rammohan, Dayananda and Phule. By privileging conceptualisation, a difference-seeking agenda figured prominently and the distinction between 'us' and 'them' was pursued consistently to develop an alternative nationalist discourse.

3. How was nation conceptualised in the early nationalist response? What are the basic ingredients of a nation according to these thinkers?

Answer by India Ebook: Read the 1 Shot Concept Above.

4.3: IGNOU Past 6 Attempts Question – Solved

Dec 2021: Examine Religio-Political ideas of Dayanand Saraswati.

June 2019: Analyse Religio-political ideas of Dayanand Saraswati.

Answer by India Ebook: While Bankim had a clear political message for the nation that lacked solidarity, **Dayananda** (1825-83) who founded the *Arya Samaj* had concerns similar to those of Rammohan. Primarily a social reformer, the latter believed that the success of the British in subjugating the Hindu society was largely due to its divisive nature and also the failure in realising its strength. If Rammohan drew upon Upanishads, Bankim upon the Gita, Dayanand while articulating his nationalist response, was inspired by Vedas. The other contrasting point that marked Dayananda off from the rest lies in the utter absence of the influence of European culture and thought on him.

Unlike them, Dayananda found the Vedic messages as most appropriate for inspiring the moribund nation, plagued by several 'ills' that could easily be cured. Seeking to construct a strong Hindu society, Dayananda, was strikingly different from other early nationalists in two specific ways: *first*, his response was essentially based on a conceptualisation that is absolutely indigenous in nature presumably because he was not exposed to the Western ideas. Unique in his approach, Dayananda therefore interrogated the processes of history in a language that added a new dimension to the early nationalist response. *Secondly*, his response was also an offshoot of a creative dialogue with the traditional scriptures, especially the Vedas - which appeared to have influenced the later Extremist leadership for its appeal to distinct civilisational characteristics of India. Unlike those who were drawn to Western liberal ideas, Dayananda was probably the only thinker of his generation to have begun a debate on the relative importance of the ancient scriptures in inspiring a nation that was divided on innumerable counts.

Dec 2021: Examine Jyotiba Phule as a social reformer.

Dec 2020: Describe the role of Jyotiba Phule as a social revolutionary.

Answer by India Ebook: Jotirao Phule (1827-9O), like Dayananda, had the dcsire for a form of social organisation that would reflect the merits and aptitudes of the individual, rather than enforcing birth as the basis both for occupation and for religious status. The play, Tritiya Ratna (The Third Eye), which he published in 1855 is a powerfull exposition of his ideology. The play is about the exploitation of an ignorant and superstitious peasant couple by a cunning Brahmin priest and their subsequent enlightenment by a Christian missionary. Three important points stand out in this play.

First, critical of Brahmin domination, he made a wider point concerning the oppressive nature of Hindu religion that, in its present form, imposed an ideological hegemony on the Shudras and by suggesting several purifying rituals, it also contributed to material impoverishment of the untouchables.

Secondly, by underlining the role of a Christain missionary who rescued the people from the cluthes of the greedy Brahmin, Phule seemed to have explored the possibility of conversion as probably the only practical device to get-out of the exploiatative Hindu religion.

Thirdly, underlying this story, there remained another major ideological point concerning the importance of education in sustaining the Brahminic hegemony in Hindu society. He was persuaded to believe that access to education, and particularly, literacy in English, conferred vital social resources on the Brahmins as a social group.

June 2021: Evaluate Raja Ram Mohan Roy as a social reformer.

Answer by India Ebook: **Rammohan Roy** was a social thinker par excellence. His role in doing away with sattee among the orthodox Brahmins was historical. By founding *Brahma Samaj*, Roy sought to articulate his belief in the Islamic notion of 'one god'. Altlzough he despised colonialism, he appeared to have endorsed the British rule presumably because of its historical role in combating the prevalent feudal forces. Not only was the British rule superior, at least, culturally than the erstwhile feudal rulers, it would also contribute to a different India by injecting the values it represented. His admiration for the British rule was based oil his faith in its role in radically altering traditional mental make-up of the Hindus.

The continued British rule, he further added, would eventually lead to the establishment of democratic institutions as in Great Britain. Like any other liberals, Roy also felt that the uncritical acceptance of British liberal values was probably the best possible means of creating democratic institutions in India. The other area for which the role of Ram Mohan was, decisive was the articulation of demand for the freedom of press. Along with his colleague, Dwarkanath Tagore, he submitted a petition to the Privy Council for the freedom of press, which he justified as essential for democratic functioning of the government.

Rammohan Roy had played a progressive role in a particular historical context. While conceptualising his historical role, Roy appeared to have privileged his experience of British colonialism over its immediate feudal past. By undermining the obvious devastating impact of foreign rule on Indian society, politics and economy, he also clearly supported one system of administration over the other rather consciously simply because of his uncritical faith in British Enlightenment in significantly trunsforming the prevalent Indian mindsets.

Dec 2018: Examine Bankim Chandra Chatterjee's ideas in shaping nationalism.

Answer by India Ebook: Read the 1 Shot Concept Above.

5. MODERATES AND EXTREMISTS: DADABHAI NAOROJI, MG RANADE AND BG TILAK

Introduction
Defining Moderates and Extremists
Moderate Ideology
Extremist Ideology
Moderate - Extremist Comparison
The Importance of Lal-Bal-Pal
The 1907 Surat Split
An Evaluation

5.1: One Shot Concepts

INTRODUCTION

The nationalist movement was articulated differently in different phases of India's freedom struggle. Apart from ideological shifts, there were noticeable differences in the social background of those who participated in the struggle against the British. For instance, the **Gandhian phase** of Indian nationalism, also known as the phase of mass nationalism, radically altered the nature of the constituencies of nationalism by incorporating the hitherto neglected sections of Indian society.

Gandhi had inaugurated a completely new phase in Indian freedom struggle can easily be shown by contrasting it with its earlier phases, namely, the _moderate and extremist_ phases. In contemporary historiography, 'the Moderate' phase begins with the formation of the Indian National Congress in **1885** and continued till the **1907** *Surat Congress* when 'the Extremists' appeared on the political scene.

The basic differences between these two groups lay in their perception of anti-British struggle and its articulation in concrete programmes. While the **Moderates** opposed the British in a strictly constitutional way the **Extremists** favoured *"a strategy of direct action"* to harm the British economic and political interests in India.

DEFINING MODERATES AND EXTREMISTS

While Moderates and Extremists constitute contrasting viewpoints, their contribution to the freedom struggle in its early phase is nonetheless significant. Moderates like Dadabhai Naoroji, Surendranath Banerji, Pherozeshah Mehta, Gopal Krishna Gokale, M. G. Ranade, were uncritical admirers of Western political values. They held the concept of equality before law, of freedom of speech and press and the principle of representative government as inherently superior to their traditional Hindu polity which they defined as 'Asiatic despotism'.

So emphatic was their faith in the British rule that they hailed its introduction in India as "a providential mission" capable of eradicating the 'mis-rule' of the past. Given the reluctance of the Crown to introduce representative institutions in India, Dadabhai Naoroji lamented that the British government in India was 'more Raj and less British'. What he meant was that though the British rule fulfilled the basic functions of Hindu kingship in preserving law and order in India, its reluctance to introduce the principle of representative government was most disappointing. So, despite their appreciation of British liberalism their admiration hardly influenced the Raj in changing the basic nature of its rule in India.

MODERATE IDEOLOGY

The moderate philosophy was most eloquently articulated by *Surendranath Banerji* (1848 - 1925) in his 1895 presidential address to the Congress. There are two points that need to be highlighted here. **First**, as evident, the Moderates identified specific roles for the Congress that sought to mobilise people in accordance with what was construed as the most appropriate goal in that context. The guiding principle was to avoid friction with the ruler. In fact, this is how G. K. Gokhale explained the birth of the Indian National congress.

Secondly, the philosophy stemmed from an uncritical faith of the early nationalists in the providential mission of the British and hence the British conquest of India was not 'a calamity' to be lamented but 'an opportunity' to be seized to 'our advantage'.

Finally, it would be wrong to dismiss the role of the Moderates in India's freedom struggle given their loyalist attitude to the rule for two reasons:

(a) there is no denying that the Moderates never launched mass agitations against the alien state in India; but by providing an ideological critique of the British rule in India keeping in view the grand ideals on which the British civilisations stood, they actually initiated a political dialogue that loomed large in course of time; and

(b) the Moderate constitutional and peaceful method of political mobilisation, if contextualised, seems to be a milestone in India's freedom struggle for it paved the ground for other kinds of anti-imperial protests once it ceased to be effective.

EXTREMIST IDEOLOGY

In contrast with the Moderates who pursued a policy of reconciliation and compromise with imperialism, the Extremists demanded time-bound programmes and policies harming the British interests in India. This new school of thought represented an alternative voice challenging the 'Moderates' compromising policies of conciliation with imperialism. Disillusioned with the Moderates, the Extremists believed in 'self reliance' and sought to achieve Swaraj through direct action. So, there were two levels at which the Extremist critique had operated.

In otherwords, the failure of Moderates in obtaining concessions for the Indians indicated the changing nature of the colonial state that had shown its true colour as soon as its political control in India was complete. So it was a level in which the Extremists articulated their opposition both to the Moderates and the British government. At another level, the Extremists also felt the need of being self-reliant economically to fight the British state that gained in strength by exploiting India's economic resources. Swadeshi was not merely an economic design but also a political slogan on which India was sought to be made strong by being self-reliant. This was an area where serious intellectual contributions were made by the exponents of *Extremism - BG Tilak, Bipin Chandra Pal, Aurobindo* among others.

There were **several factors** that had contributed to the disillusionment of the Extremists with the Moderates. *First*, the growing government atrocities, especially in the wake of the **1905 Bengal partition agitation**, clearly revealed the inadequacies of the constitutional and peaceful means. *Secondly*, the uncritical acceptance of **Western enlightenment of the Moderates** was also **rejected** as a sign of emotional bankruptcy, especially, given the rich heritage of Indian civilisation. *Thirdly*, the **recurrence of famine** and the lackadaisical attitude of the British government brought out the exploitative nature of colonial power in clear terms.

As evident, by the early part of the 20th century and especially in the context of the 1905 Bengal partition agitation, the Moderates lost credibility since their anti-itnperial strategies failed to gain what they aspired for. Moreover, their faith in the British liberalism did not work to their advantage and it dawned on the later nationalists, paritularly the Extremists, that the colonial power in India drew more on exploitation and less on the basic tenets of liberalism.

MODERATE - EXTREMIST COMPARISON   IGNOU Book Q.1

The *distinction* between the **Moderates** and **Extremists** is based on serious differences among themselves in their respective approaches to the British Empire. Based on their perception, the Moderates hailed the British rule as most beneficial in contrast with what India had confronted before the arrival of the British. Until the *1905 Bengal partition*, the Moderate philosophy was based on loyalty to 'the Empire that had shown signs of cracks in the aftermath of atrocities, meted out to those opposing Curzon's canonical design of causing a fissure among the Indians by highlighting their religious schism.

Opposed to the Moderate stance, the Extremists always considered the British rule as a curse that could never render justice to the governed in India. Not only did they challenge the British government for its 'evil' design against the Indians, they also criticised the Moderates for having misled the nationalist aspirations in a way that was clearly defeating.

Another difference between the Moderates and Extremists was based on their respective approaches to the outcome of the nationalist intervention. While the Moderates stood for the attainment of 'self government' through gradual reforms, the Extremists insisted on complete Swaraj. In other words, the model of self-government, as evident in the dominion of Canada and Australia, appeared to be an ideal form of government for India.

The Extremists were not hesitant in championing 'violence', if necessary, to advance the cause of the nation while the Moderates favoured constitutional and peaceful methods as most appropriate to avoid direct friction with the ruler.

5.2: IGNOU Book Exercise – Solved

1. What are the distinctive features of Moderate and Extremist philosophy?

Answer by India Ebook: Read the 1 Shot Concept Above.

2. What are the factors that contributed to the growth of Extremists in Indian nationalism?

Answer by India Ebook: The failure of Moderates in obtaining concessions for the Indians indicated the changing nature of the colonial state that had shown its true colour as soon as its political control in India was complete. So it was a level in which the Extremists articulated their opposition both to the Moderates and the British government. At another level, the Extremists also felt the need of being self-reliant economically to fight the British state that gained in strength by exploiting India's economic resources. Swadeshi was not merely an economic design but also a political slogan on which India was sought to be made strong by being self-reliant. This was an area where serious intellectual contributions were made by the exponents of *Extremism - BG Tilak, Bipin Chandra Pal, Aurobindo* among others.

There were **several factors** that had contributed to the disillusionment of the Extremists with the Moderates. *First*, the growing government atrocities, especially in the wake of the **1905 Bengal partition agitation**, clearly revealed the inadequacies of the constitutional and peaceful means. *Secondly*, the uncritical acceptance of **Western enlightenment of the Moderates** was also **rejected** as a sign of emotional bankruptcy, especially, given the rich heritage of Indian civilisation. *Thirdly*, the **recurrence of famine** and the lackadaisical attitude of the British government brought out the exploitative nature of colonial power in clear terms.

As evident, by the early part of the 20th century and especially in the context of the 1905 Bengal partition agitation, the Moderates lost credibility since their anti-itnperial strategies failed to gain what they aspired for. Moreover, their faith in the British liberalism did not work to their advantage and it dawned on the later nationalists, paritularly the Extremists, that the colonial power in India drew more on exploitation and less on the basic tenets of liberalism.

3. How do you account for the split between the Moderates and Extremists?

Answer by India Ebook: The nationalist movement was articulated differently in different phases of India's freedom struggle. Apart from ideological shifts, there were noticeable differences in the social background of those who participated in the struggle against the British. For instance, the **Gandhian phase** of Indian nationalism, also known as the phase of mass nationalism, radically altered the nature of the constituencies of nationalism by incorporating the hitherto neglected sections of Indian society.

Gandhi had inaugurated a completely new phase in Indian freedom struggle can easily be shown by contrasting it with its earlier phases, namely, the *moderate and extremist* phases. In contemporary historiography, 'the Moderate' phase begins with the formation of the Indian National Congress in **1885** and continued till the **1907** *Surat Congress* when 'the Extremists' appeared on the political scene.

The basic differences between these two groups lay in their perception of anti-British struggle and its articulation in concrete programmes. While the **Moderates** opposed the British in a strictly constitutional way the **Extremists** favoured *"a strategy of direct action"* to harm the British economic and political interests in India.

The *moderate philosophy* was most eloquently articulated by **Surendranath Banerji** (1848 - 1925) in his 1895 presidential address to the Congress. The failure of Moderates in obtaining concessions for the Indians indicated the changing nature of the colonial state that had shown its true colour as soon as its political control in India was complete. So it was a level in which the *Extremists* articulated their opposition both to the Moderates and the British government.

5.3: IGNOU Past 6 Attempts Question – Solved

Dec 2021: Compare and contrast the ideology of the Moderates and Extremists during the nationalist movement.

Answer by India Ebook: Same as Q.1 of Above.

Dec 2020: What are the contributions of the moderates and extremists to India's freedom?

Answer by India Ebook: Same as Q.7 of Above.

6. HINDUISM: SWAMI VIVEKANANDA AND SRI AUROBINDO GHOSH

Introduction
Renaissance of Hinduism and the Role of Sri Ramakrishna Mission
Swami Vivekananda's Philosophy of Neo-Vedanta
Swami Vivekananda on Nationalism
- Swami Vivekananda on Democracy
- Swami Vivekananda on Social Change

Transition of Hinduism: From Vivekananda to Sri Aurobindo
- Sri Aurobindo on Renaissance of Hinduism
- Sri Aurobindo on Evil Effects of British Rule

Sri Aurobindo's Critique of Political Moderates in India
- Sri Aurobindo on the Essence of Politics
- Sri Aurobindo on Nationalism
- Sri Aurobindo on Passive Resistance
- Theory of Passive Resistance
- Methods of Passive Resistance

Sri Aurobindo on the Indian Theory of State
- Political Ideas of Sri Aurobindo - A Critical Study

6.1: One Shot Concepts

INTRODUCTION

In 19th century, India camc under the British rule. Due to the spread of modern education and growing public activities, there developed social awakening in India. The religion of Hindus wns very harshly criticized by the Christian missionaries and the British historians but at the same time, researches carried out by the Orientalist scholars revealed to the world, the glorious tradition of the Hindu religion. The Hindus responded to this by initiating reforms in their religion and by establishing new public associations to spread their ideas of reform and social development among the people. They wanted to give new birth to Hinduism.

The process of renaissance of Hinduism started with Raja Ram Mohan Roy and it was further developed by the Asya Samaj of Swami Dayanand, the Prarthana Samaj and the Satyashodhak Samaj of Jotiba Phule, Sri Ramkrishna Mission, founded by Swami Vivekananda, played a key role in renaissance and reformation of Hindu society. There was a new interpretation of Vedanta philosophy and Swami Vivekananda and Sri Aurobindo Ghosh were two major interpreters of Neo-Vedanta philosophy. They were of the opinion that Neo-Vedanta philosophy would increase cultural strength of Hinduism and pave the way for the growth of nationalism in modern India. They interpreted Indian nationalism in the context of reformation and rejuvenation of Hinduism.

RENAISSANCE OF HINDUISM AND THE ROLE OF SRI RAMAMRISHNA MISSION   IGNOU Book Q.4

RamaKrishna Mission played a key role in the renaissance of Hinduism. It was established by *Swami Vivekananda*. It was named after his teacher Sri Ramakrishna Paramhamsa. Ramakrishna (1836-86) was a son of soil and never lost his rustic simplicity, He was a mystic who preached self-less devotion of God and ultimate absorption in him. He personified the rebirth of ancient tradition in the midst of growing westernisation.

He preached the people to follow the path of self-less devotion and claimed that service of man was service of God. He asked his disciples to live pure life, free af passions, desires, hatred and pride. He condemned no one and saw good in all. It was his firm belief that the religions of the world were not contradictory but were various phases of one eternal religion.

His disciple Swami Vivekananda established the Ramakrishna Mission to serve the people. He wanted to find a new path of progress for Hinduism because he was not happy with the reform movements as they were imitations of the western methods. He had **three alternatives** before him. *First*, to follow the path shown by Raja Ram Mohan Roy and join Brahmo Samaj, *Secondly*, to follow thk path of total renunciation and go to Himalayas to atfain the goal of liberation. *Thirdly*, to follow the path of service to the society and to create social awakening in the minds of the people about resuscitation of the Indian society.

Vivekananda chose the **third path** and told the Indians to see Narayana in the form of a poor beggar dying of starvation. Thus, for Vivekananda the Ramakrishna Mission should stand for selfless service of the people, ceaseless efforts to find truth and thereby for reawakening of the spirit of

India. During Vivekananda's life time and after his death, Sri Ramakrishna Mission played a key role in the renaissance of Hinduism.

SWAMI VIVEKANANDA'S PHILOSOPHY OF NEO-VEDANTA

IGNOU Book Q.5

Vedanta philosophy was one of the most important ancient philosophies of India which believed that God alone was real and the visible world was unreapand the absorption of individual soul in the one supreme soul was the goal of every human being. That was called liberation and it could be achieved with the help of true knowledge. Raja Ram Mohan Roy was a supporter of non-dualistic monism. He expounded the concept of fatherhood of God and the brotherhood of man. But Vivekananda followed the Vedanta preached by his teacher which was rooted in the traditional Indian wisdom of Bhakti tradition, He did not believe in the path of renunciation and asked people to perform their duties in the spirit of self-lessness.

There were **three** important principles of *Neo-Vedanta philosophy* of **Vivekananda**. They were as follows:

- Vedanta believed in the oneness between God and man and the solidarity of Universe.
- It did not stand for a life of renunciation but stood for self-less action in the services of humanity. Hence, service of man should be considered as service of Cod.
- It propagated the principle of universal tolerance and believed that different religious faiths were different paths to reach the goal of liberation.

Thus; for Swami Vivekananda, Neo-Vedanta philosophy stood 'for service, sacrifice and freedom. He did not want the Neo-Vedantists to remain inactive but to work for the awakening of the masses. He wanted young Indians to dedicate themselves in the cause of resurgence of India.

SWAMI VIVEKAMANDA ON NATIONALISM   *IGNOU Book Q.6*

Swami Vivekananda is considered as one of the prophets of the Indian nationalism because he tried to awaken Indian people who were lying in deep slumber. He wanted to see the emergence of a strong and self-confident India which would give the message of the Vedanta to the world. He maintained that the Indians should be proud of their history, culture and religion and should try their level best to reform them - in the light of the demands of time. The awakening of the spirit of India was the goal for young people. Hence, he asked them to "arise, awake and stop not till the goal is reached."

Vivekananda was of the opinion that the national regeneration of India would begin when people became fearless and started demanding their rights. Also, he asked the Indians to develop solidarity and oneness of the spirit by the eradication of social evils, superstitions and caste-arrogance. He was of the opinion that caste system divided the Indian society into classes and created the feeling of inferiority, and superiority among them.

He held that though there was a variety of races, languages, religions and cultures in India, there existed a common ground between Indian people. There was a common religious tradition which could be depended upon to build national spirit. India should be of one mind and of one resolve. Hence, we must revive the whole of India. India must conquer the world not with the help of gun, but with the help of spirituality.

For the growth of national spirit in India, independence of mind was necessary. India should expose herself to the outside world but she should not get scared of any one because her freedom would come through heroism and bravery. Indians should be proud of their country and declare that all Indians, despite their different castes and religions, are brothers. Thus in **Vivekananda's theory of nationalism**, there were four important **components** which were as follows:

- There was unity and oneness of the Indian people despite their outward diversity.
- It was necessary to remove caste differences to inculcate the spirit of social solidarity.
- There war similarity in the teachings of different religions and India consisted of all religious communities.
- National spirit in India could be developed by young people by devoting their life to social service and national awakening.

➢ **Swami Vivekananda on Democracy**

Vivekananda was a great advocate of democracy and he wanted to awaken the young people to establish free and democratic government in

India. For him, the principle of liberty was important because he held that there could not be growth in society as well as that of an individual without liberty. He said that every one should have liberty of thought, discussion, food, marriage and dress. He wanted to democratise the Indian society by abolishing caste privileges, by opposing cunning of priest craft and social tyranny.

Vivekananda was a supporter of equality of all men and pleaded for the abolition of caste and class privileges. He thought that the spirit of equality in India could be inculcated through the spread of knowledge and education. Caste system was a hindrance to the development of India into a strong nation. He held that in democracy, power rested with the people. He was of the view that for the democratisation of the country, the western thinkers tried to perfect the political and social order but the Eastern thinkers laid more stress on perfection of individual. For, sound social and political institutions were ultimately rooted in the goodness of individuals. For him, religious tolerance was crucial for the growth of democracy because that alone could promote the cause of liberty, equality and fraternity.

> **Swami Vivekananda on Social Change**   IGNOU Book Q.7

Vivekananda wanted an overall development of India and the eradication of poverty and degeneration of the people. He was an opponent of aristocracy and feudalism. He pleaded for bridging the gap between the rich and the poor.

Vivekananda's theory of social change was based on the Indian concept of history. It was a theory of political cycle that visualised periodic and circular change in the regimes on the basis of law of change, with the help of historical evidences from the history of Greece, Rome and India. He held that in every individual, there prevailed **three qualities** of *Sattva* (Knowledge) *Rajas* (Valour) and *Tamas* (ignorance) and in every society and in every civilisation, there existed four classes of the people. All societies which had developed division of labour had **four classes** of *Brahmins, Kshatriyas, Vaishyas* and *Shudras*. According to Swami Vivekananda, on the basis of historical examples and law of nature, each of this, class in every society governed the country, one after another in succession.

Vivekananda was of the opinion that in the first stage of human development, in almost all ancient civilisations of the world, the power was in the hands of the Brahmin or a priest. He ruled with the help of magic. His power was overthrown by the Kshatriyas or warriors who formed monarchical or oligarchic governments. But the power of this class was overthrown by the Vaishyas or traders. In most of the modern nations, such as England, the power of controlling society was in the hands of Vaishyas, who amassed wealth by carrying out commerce and trade.

According to Vivekananda, as per the law of nature, wherever there was an awakening of new and stronger life, there it tried to conquer and take the place of the old and the decaying. Nature favoured the dying of the unfit and the survival of the fittest. The power of the Kshatriyas was brought down because of its dictatorship. He maintained that the real power of the society rested with the Shudras who produced wealth with the help of their labour power. Thus, in the political theory of Vivekananda, the awakening and freedom of India was synchronised with the rise of Shudras and workers and peasants to political power. He was a supporter of nationalism and provided the basis of Neo-Vedanta to it. He used religion and culture in the cause of nationalism.

TRANSITION OF HINDUISM: FROM VIVEKANANDA TO SRI AUROBINDO

In the social and political ideas of Swami Vivekananda, we had seen the rise of Hinduism and Indian nationalism. New Hinduism became the tool of national consciousness in India. But this consciousness was broad enough to include Muslim, Parsee, Christian and other minorities in India. In the beginning of the 20th century, nationalism became more aggressive and anti-colonial. Sri Aurobindo Ghosh was instrumental in giving radical content to nationalism in India.

The Political career of Aurobindo Ghosh began in the last decade of 19th century as he spent 13 years of his life in England to get the best English education. He returned to India and studied history and philosophy. In the process, he became one of the authentic exponents of Hinduism and Hindu philosophy. He joined the extremist group in the Congress and took a leading role in the anti-partition movement in Bengal.

During this period, he mobilised people through speeches and writings. He was a leading member of the radical group in the Congress party. The British government tried to suppress the Swadeshi movement. Tilak and Aurobindo were arrested, Lala Lajpat Rai was deported and many were put behind the bars, Along with Aurobindo, his revolutionary brother Barinder was arrested on the charges of sedition. In the trial, Aurobindo was acquitted but Barinder was sent to gallows. In the jail, he had certain spiritual and mystical experiences and as a result, he decided to leave politics and concentrate on the life of philosophy and Yoga.

In a brief political career, Aurobindo carried forward the process of the renaissance of Hinduism on the basis of Vedanta and deepened the concept of spiritual nationalism.

> **Sri Aurobindo on Renaissance of Hinduism**   IGNOU Book Q.8

As we have seen, Sri Aurobindo was a prominent figure in the renaissance of Hinduism and he wanted to complete the task left incomplete by Swami Vivekananda and Bankimchandra Chatterjee. Aurobindo carried forward the development of Neo-Vedanta and declared that the true message of Vedanta was selfless action or Karma Yoga. In the theory of Karma Yoga, a person was enjoined to perform his duties without aspiring far the fruits thereof, The Geeta taught us to fight against injustice because life is a series of struggles.

Aurobindo was of the opinion that there was a need of the renaissance of Hinduism which called for the awakening of the Indian soul which was in deep slumber. It could achieve its: glory through the philosophy of Vedanta which gave more importance to spirituality than to science. The West glorified science but science is a light within a limited room and not the sun that which illumines the world. The spirit of every human heart had to be awakened to revive the glory of Hinduism. Hinduism should change the rags of the past so that its beauty might be restored. It must alter its bodily appearance so that her soul might be newly expressed.

According to Sri Aurobindo, the goal of new Hinduism was to pave the way for emergence of Indian nationalism and to harmonise the world and the spirit. He held that the genius of the Hindu was not for pure action but for thought and aspiration realised in action.

➢ Sri Aurobindo on Evil Effects of British Rule   IGNOU Book Q.9

Aurobindo was a harsh critic of the British rule in India. He did not agree with the opinion of the moderates that it was a divine dispensation. He said that it was a curse for the majority of the Indian people because the foreign rule in India sapped moral and mental energies of the Indian people.

The ***British rule ruined*** the economy of India and did not allow the latter to develop as an independent nation. It disorganised the Indians into a crowd, with no centre of strength or means of resistance. Her industries and trade were ruined and agriculture devastated. The British government in India was the worst type of bureaucratic despotism motivated by plunder and domination. India was held in subjection for the benefit of the British ruling classes. The British claim of a good government was false and a good and efficient government was no substitute for self-government and freedom.

It was the contention of Aurobindo that the spirit of India could be free only by securing complete independence of the country. Freedom from foreign rule was an inalienable right of the people. The ***evil effects*** of the **British rule** could be eradicated only by overthrowing it. Its continuance would further worsen the situation in India.

SRI AUROBINDO'S CRITIQUE OF POLITICAL MODERATES IN INDIA

When Aurobindo Ghosh entered Indian politics, it was dominated by the moderate leaders who were of the view that British rule in India was a divine dispensation. Aurobindo was highly critical of their approach to politics. Hence, he wrote a series of articles in the 'Indu Prakash' of Pune under the title 'New Lamps for Old' and severely criticised the politics of petitions and prayers of the moderate leaders.

Aurobindo said that the Congress leaders had very narrow and limited ideals. The Congress was selfishly frigid of social development and awakening of the masses and organically infirm. It was unaware of deeper facts; therefore, it did not articulate the popular opinion of the entire Indian people.

Aurobindo argued that during Ram Mohan Roy's period, politics of prayers and petition was the only possible policy, but it was wrong to continue it even in the later years. He pleaded for the adoption of new and strong methods. He wrote that the ideas that governed the country were pgrely western; hence, they could not seize the attention of the people. The Indians should realise that both the liberals and the conservatives were supporters of the continuance of the British rule in India; therefore, the Congress should not expect much from John Morley - the liberal leader - because he was an ardent supporter of imperialism.

He called for a complete change in the policy of the Congress party because under the moderate leadership, the Congress confused sufferance with freedom and favour of foreign despotism with the right of citizenship. If the Congress did not understand it, it would remain unfit for freedom and the standing hindrance to the country's freedom. He pleaded for the adoption of new policies and programmes to replace the politics of supplication carried out by the moderates.

> ### Sri Aurobindo on the Essence of Politics

After the partition of Bengal, there was a tremendous upheaval in the country and a large number of the people joined the Swadeshi movement led by the radical group of the Congress party. Aurobindo joined Tilak, Bipinchandra Pal and Lala Lajpat Rai to popularise the programme of the party. He was a philosopher of new party. He wanted the Congress to be with people, speak in their language, identity itself with the wishes and aspirations of the - people and Indianise the movement in the true sense of the term.

Aurobindo aided that Swaraj, Swadeshi, national education and boycott were *four methods* of the new party:

- For him, **'Swaraj'** meant complete independence because he argued that a political agitation was not launched to secure a few seats in bureaucracy and in assembly but to secure right of self-government to the people.
- *Swadeshi* meant using the products that were manufactured in our country only.
- *National education* stood for imparting education to Indians that suited to their temperament, needs and culture.
- *Boycott* meant not using the products manufactured in England.

All these four methods were necessary to train the people in national spirit and to be architects of liberty. Thus, for Aurobindo, new politics stood for self-development and self-help. He hoped that it would inculcate the spirit of nationalism in people.

➢ Sri Aurobindo on Nationalism — IGNOU Book Q.1

Sri Aurobindo Ghosh was considered as a prophet of the Indian nationalism. Along with Bankimchandra, Tilak and Dayanand, he developed the theory of nationalism in India. Through their self-less work, the forces of nationalism were released.

Sri Aurobindo's theory of nationalism was based on Vedanta philosophy which saw unity and oneness in man and God. There was an essential unity in India despite the existence of the outward differences because the spirit of unity and oneness pervaded it. For her rejuvenation,

India needed "Shakti' or the power that was physical, moral, material and spiritual. The power or strength of a nation depended on the unity of her nation. Aurobindo was critical of those people who claimed that due to cultural, racial and linguistic diversity and divisions in the Indian society, India could never become a nation. He pointed out that if we carefully studied the history of Europe and England of the last two centuries, we would realise that their condition was no way different from India.

Aurobindo pointed out that there were certain essential elements in the formation of nationality. These essential elements were geographical unity, common past, a powerful common interest impelling towards unity and certain favourable political conditions which enabled the impulse to realise itself in an organised government. Aurobindo recognised the importance of villages in the Indian life and pointed out that unlike in the West, where the city was the Centre of all political action, in India vfllage was the backbone of national persistence. Indian villages were democratic, autonomous and selfgoverning. Therefore, regeneration of the village was important for the regeneration of India.

Aurobindo's concept of nationalism was based on the philosophy of Vedanta which stood for unity between God and man. He used Hindu religious ideas and symbols. He realised that the ideal of Indian nationalism was largely Hindu in character but he pointed out that this nationalism was wide enough to include the Muslim, his culture and traditions. He said that the Hindu should win Swaraj for himself as well as for the Muslim. A large part of his theory of nationalism was based on awakening the dormant spirit of nationalism that was latent in the soul of India. The struggle against the foreign rule would enable it to achieve self-realisation.

➤ Sri Aurobindo on Passive Resistance

The new party of the radicals wanted to use new methods against the government to secure political rights for the Indian people. Aurobindo thought that the method of passive resistance, which was used by the Irish nationalists, would be ideal for India. Hence, he developed theory of passive resistance in a series of articles published in the weekly called 'Bande Mataram".

➤ Theory of Passive Resistance

According to Sri Aurobindo, for a subject country, the attainment of political independence was its highest goal. But there were different means to attain that goal. In India, for Indian patriots, three alternative means were available to win Swaraj and they were as follows:

i) the method of prayers and petitions.

ii) the method of armed revolt.

iii) the method of self-development and passive resistance.

➤ Methods of Passive Resistance

The essence of passive resistance was to challenge the authority of the state by following non-violent means because under the present circumstances armed conflict or a violent aggressive resistance in the form of sabotage, assassinations and terrorism was not possible and desirable.

One of the major benefits of passive resistance was that through this method, we would be in a position to involve people and let them learn methods of struggle and sufferings. It would train the Indians in heroic actions and boost their morale. It would bring pressure on the government to keep the promises it had made to people.

According to Aurobindo, passive resistance worked on two levels. At the first level, it encouraged the people to pursue the methods of self-development such as Swadeshi, and national education and at the second level, it sought to exert pressure on the government to concede the demands of the people. According to him, in the passive resistance, the following measures would be undertaken to achieve success:

- Refusal to assit the government.
- Refusal to pay taxes to the government.
- Boycotting the products manufactured in the foreign countries.
- Boycottitlg the government schools, colleges and law courts.
- Starting our own schools, colleges and arbitration courts to train people in the method of self help and national independence.

SRI AUROBINDO ON THE INDIAN THEORY OF STATE

IGNOU Book Q.3

Sri Aurobindo renounced active politics in 1910 and left for Pondicherry to pursue his spiritual goals. All attempts to bring him back to national politics did not succeed. In the second phase of his life, Aurobindo emerged as a great sage and a philosopher and received worldwide respect. He became the authentic representative of Indian wisdom. He wrote in 1947, a book explaining the spirit and form of the Indian polity. According to Aurobiado, ancient Indian thinkers developed an Indian model of state building which was democratic in character in the sense that it allowed communal freedom and selfgovernment and autonomy to the village and the community. It was a synthesis of communal autonomies of village, town, caste, guild and family. The state was a means of holding together and synthesised free and living organic systems and autonomies into fret: and living organisms. Indians successfully struck the right balance between stability and change. It was an organic totality of social existence. Ancient Indian system had a capacity to renew itself.

According to Aurobindo, the Indians did not want to establish a mechanical state that laid exaggerated dependence on legislation, administration and force. The Western idea of state was artificial and the state in the West was imposed upon the people. The Indian system was flexible and was built up from within. The Western state was based on a rigid uniformity but in the Indian system, new elements were harmonised without destroying the original elements and existing institutions. It was a creation of practical reason and the common experience of communal self-government.

6.2: IGNOU Book Exercise – Solved

1. Discuss Sri Aurobindo's theory of Nationalism.

Answer by India Ebook: Read the 1 Shot Concept Above.

2: Describe in brief the methods of passive resistance advocated by Aurobindo.

Answer by India Ebook: The new party of the radicals wanted to use new methods against the government to secure political rights for the Indian people. Aurobindo thought that the method of passive resistance, which was used by the Irish nationalists, would be ideal for India. Hence, he developed theory of passive resistance in a series of articles published in the weekly called 'Bande Mataram".

According to Sri Aurobindo, for a subject country, the attainment of political independence was its highest goal. But there were different means to attain that goal. In India, for Indian patriots, three alternative means were available to win Swaraj and they were as follows:

i) the method of prayers and petitions.

ii) the method of armed revolt.

iii) the method of self-development and passive resistance.

The essence of passive resistance was to challenge the authority of the state by following non-violent means because under the present circumstances armed conflict or a violent aggressive resistance in the form of sabotage, assassinations and terrorism.

According to Aurobindo, passive resistance worked on two levels. At the first level, it encouraged the people to pursue the methods of self-development such as Swadeshi, and national education and at the second level, it sought to exert pressure on the government to concede the demands of the people. According to him, in the passive resistance, the following measures would be undertaken to achieve success:

- Refusal to assit the government.
- Refusal to pay taxes to the government.
- Boycotting the products manufactured in the foreign countries.
- Boycottitlg the government schools, colleges and law courts.
- Starting our own schools, colleges and arbitration courts to train people in the method of self help and national independence.

3. Discuss the salient features of Aurobindo's theory of state.

Answer by India Ebook: Read the 1 Shot Concept Above.

4. Discuss briefly the main features of renaissance of Hinduism.

Answer by India Ebook: Read the 1 Shot Concept Above.

5. Write a short note on the Neo-Vedanta philosophy of Swami Vivekananda.

Answer by India Ebook: Read the 1 Shot Concept Above.

6. Discuss briefly Swami Vivekananda's views on nationalism.

Answer by India Ebook: Read the 1 Shot Concept Above.

7. Briefly state the salient features of Swami Vivekananda's theory of social change.

Answer by India Ebook: Read the 1 Shot Concept Above.

8. What were Sri Aurobindo's views on the renaissance of Hinduism?

Answer by India Ebook: Read the 1 Shot Concept Above.

9. What were the evil effects of the British rule, according to Aurobindo?

Answer by India Ebook: Read the 1 Shot Concept Above.

6.3: IGNOU Past 6 Attempts Question - Solved

June 2021: Examine Sri Aurobindo's Vision of Nationalism.

Answer by India Ebook: Same as Q.1 of Above.

Dec 2020: Examine Swami Vivekananda's ideas on social change.

Answer by India Ebook: Same as Q.7 of Above.

June 2020: Examine Sri Aurobindo's critique of Political moderates in India.

Answer by India Ebook: Refer 1 Shot Concept Above.

June 2019: What were the evil effects of the British rule according to Aurobindo?

Answer by India Ebook: Same as Q.9 of Above.

7. HINDUTVA: V. D. SAVARKAR AND M. S. GOLWALKAR

Introduction
Background of the Rise of Hindu Nationalist Ideology
  - Political Career of V D Savarkar
  - Savarkar's Views on Social Change
V D Savarkar on Social Reforms
Hindu Nationalism of V D Savarkar
  - Hindutva as Cultural Nationalism
  - Hindu Nation and Indian State
  - Hindu Nationalism of V D Savarkar - A Critical Study
  - Growth of Hindutva and the Rashtriya Swayam Sevak Sangh (RSS)
Hindu Nationalism of M S Golwalkar
  - Nation as Motherland
  - Territorial Nationalisni Rejected
  - Hindu Nationalism and Minorities
Golwalkar on Social Organisation
Political Ideas of M S Golwalkar
  - Three World Views of Change
  - Negative and Positive Hindutva
  - Hindu Nationalism of M S Golwalkar - A Critical Study

7.1: One Shot Concepts

INTRODUCTION

The ideology of 'Hindutva' was essentially the ideology of Hindu nationalism. The *first* prominent exponent of ***Hindu nationalist ideology*** was **Mr. V. D. Savarkar**. He wrote a **book** called *'Hindutva'* in **1924** to explain the basic principles of Hindu nationalism. In **1925**, the **R.S.S.** or the ***Rashtriya Swayam Sevak Sangh*** was formed to protect the Hindus from the Muslim aggression. The **R.S.S.** was established by **Dr. Keshav Baliram Hedgewar.**

In the subsequent period, Savarkar and the R.S.S. propagated the Hindu nationalist ideology against the ideology of the composite Indian nationalism expounded by Mahatma Gandhi and the Congress. **Mr. M. S. Golwalkar**, who succeeded Hedgewar expounded the Hindu nationalist ideology of the R.S.S. The **basic difference** between **Hinduism** and ***Hindutva*** is that Hinduism stands for Hindu religion, but Hindutva is a political ideology that wants to establish Hindu nation in

India. Hinduism does not have any political agenda, but Hindutva has a specific political agenda.

BACKGROUND OF THE RISE OF HINDU NATIONALIST IDEOLOGY   IGNOU Book Q.1

After the *failure of Non-cooperation movement*, there was growth of communal and separatist ideas both among Hindus and Muslims. Both of them claimed that their ideology was not a communal ideology but it was a true nationalist ideology which took into consideration the culture and religion of the people. After 1922-23, the followers of Lokmanya Tilak started supporting the Hindutva movement. Along with them the newly educated Hindu middle class also supported it. The Mopala revolt in Kerala created a lot of unrest in the Hindu community.

The *main arguments* of the **Hindutva** supporters were as follows:

i) In the past, the Hindus suffered many a defeat and lost their independence to the foreign invaders because of lack of unity. They had numbers, valour and resources at their command but they faced defeat due to lack of unity.

ii) The Hindus had been losing their numbers due to the aggressive proselitisation by the Christian missionaries and the Muslims. As a result, in a long time they would be reduced to a minority in their land of birth. Hence, in order to maintain the level of Hindu population, the Shuddhi and Samghatana movements should be launched.

iii) There was a need to protect the political interests of Hindus because the British government was hostile to them; the Muslims aggressively prsued their separatist agenda and the congress under the false notion of secularism was betraying the cause of Hindus.

In India, we could see the emergence of two traditions of Hindutva, the first tradition was led by V. D. Savarkar and the second tradition was led by M.S. Golwalkar. Though both the traditions professed their allegiance to the ideology of Hindutva, their emphasis and methods differed.

> **Political Career of V. D. Savarkar**

V. D. Savarkar (1883-1966) was a charismatic leader, who played a significant role in the freedom struggle of India. For his revolutionary activities he was sent to Andamans in 1911 and was brought back to India in 1922. Subsequently, he was kept confined to Ratnagiri town from 1923-1937. During this period, he suffered great hardships and made countless sacrifices in the cause of freedom of the country. There were two phases in the ideological development of Savarkar.

In the first phase of his life, he was influenced by the philosophy of the Italian nationalist Joseph Mazzini and supported the concept of the composite Indian nationalism, which was not different from the nationalism of Aurobindo and Tilak. During this period, religion played an important role in his concept of nationalism, but it did not exclude any religious community from it. But in the second phase of his career after 1922-23, Savarkar became the supporter of Hindu nationalism. After his release from the confinement in 1937, he joined the Hindu Mahasabha and became its President from 1938 to 1945.

> **Savarkar's Views on Social Change**   IGNOU Book Q.2

V. D. Savarkar was a product of renaissance in the Western India and in his early days he was influenced by the philosophy of **Gopal Ganesh Agarkar**, a rationalist philosopher. Agarkar was deeply influenced by the ideas of *Herbert Spencer*, *J. Bentham* and *J.S.Mill*. From the **European** philosophical tradition, he borrowed three important ideas:

i) In nature and in all human societies, the principle of life struggle determined the course of action because in this life struggle, the fittest survived and those who could not stand the struggle got eliminated.

ii) Violence was in-built in the creation of nature and-the nature abhorred absolute non-violence. But due to gradual development of human beings, both violence and non-violence got intertwined. Hence, in this difficult life, man should acquire strength and power to overcome the problems he faced.

iii) There was no absolute morality in the world. Morality or immorality of a particular action was ultimately determined by the factors such as time, space and object.

Savarkar was a supporter of positivist epistemology and accepted the direct evidence of the senses as the only valid source of knowledge. He rejected the sanctity of religious scriptures and maintained that all religious scriptures were man-made and their teaching could not be applied to all societies in all times. He rejected otherworldly philosoplly of Shankara and Ramanuja and discounted otherworldly pursuits of man.

Thus, in *Savarkar's theory* of **social change**, the principle of life struggle played an important role. For him, reason, science and technology were important to bring about the change in the society.

V. D. SAVARKAR ON SOCIAL REFORMS   IGNOU Book Q.3

Savarkar was a great supporter of social reforms and he exhorted the Hindus to accept modern practices based on science and reason and reject the religious superstitions and customs which were standing hindrance to the social progress. Savarkar was a critic of caste system. He held that both *'Chaturvarna'* and *caste system* proved very disastrous for the unity of Hindu society. The 'Chatruvarna' was based not on any scientific criterion, but was a creation of scriptures and age old beliefs. It gave birth to inhuman practice of untouchability.

Historically, Hindus constantly faced defeats at the hands of invaders because of the caste system. The untouchability was a distortion and it was wrong to consider any human being as untouchable. It militated against the spirit of human brotherhood.

Savarkar wanted the Hindus to reject blind faith in the Vedas and customs and tried to acquire material strength. They should accept the supremacy of machines and technology and break all bonds of blind faith and customs. It was incumbent upon Hindus to weed out all the defects in their society so that they could emerge as a strong nation in the world.

For Savarkar, social reforms, rationalism and science were needed for the development of a Hindu society which would enable it to acquire the necessary strength. He said that in modern times, nation was accepted as a viable unit for human beings. In the international politics, conflict and competition was raging between different nations of the world. In the international politics, language of strength was understood. Hence, Hindus should acquire strength through the pursuit of science and technology, so that they could protect their national interest as well as self-interest.

HINDU NATIONALISM OF V. D. SAVARKAR

Savarkar was the first systematic exponent of the Hindu nationalism. He elaborately described his theory of Hindutva in his book 'Hindutva' published in 1924. In the process of developing his concept of Hindu nationalism, he rejected some of the arguments of territorial nationalism. He held that the existence of a mere territory did not make nation but nation was made by the people who constituted themselves as a political community, bound together by cultural affinities and traditions.

➤ Hindutva as Cultural Nationalism

Savarkar was a supporter of cultural nationalism. He was of the opinion that identity formation was the essence of nationalism. India had received such identity from the Hindu religion. This identity was evolved over a long period of time. Despite having outward differences, the Hindus were internally bound together by cultural, religious, social, linguistic and historical affinities.

Savarkar argued that it was cultural, racial and religious unity that counted more in the formation of the nation. While defining nation, Savarkar wrote that nation meant a political community which had occupied a contiguous and adequate territory and developed independent national identity. This community was internally organised and was bound together by cultural and racial affinities. He held that the Hindus had become nation because they possessed all these characteristics.

Savarkar was of the opinion that Hindus constituted nation because they had developed close affinities with the land bound by Himalayas to the Indian Ocean and the Indus River. Hindus considered India as their fatherland and holy land. Savarkar tried to show that those people constituted nation who considered India as fatherland and holy land. In this definition, Savarkar effectively excluded those people wlio did not consider India as their holy land - because their sacred religious places were not situated in India. For him, Hindu nationalism stood for the unity of all Hindus.

➤ Hindu Nation and Indian Siate　　　　　IGNOU Book Q.5

Savarkar wanted the Hindu nation to be strong and powerful so that India could survive as an independent strong nation in the ferocious life struggle that was going on between different countries of the world.

For Savarkar, Hindus as a community, formed nation. Hence, he laid stress on the principle of exclusion. He excludcd Muslims and Christians from the Indian nation because they did not consider India as a holy land because their sacred religious places were situated outside India. Hence, he laid emphasis on the difference between Hindus and Muslims. Therefore, he wrote that everything that was common among us weakened our resolve to oppose them; Hindus were constantly fighting against Non-Hindus to save their community. Hence, he launched the

Shuddhi movement to reconvert the converted Hindus to Hinduism and to purge Marathi language of Arabic and Persian words.

Savarkar held that nation was a cultural category but state was a political category. All Hindus were the members of the nation. Non-Hindus might not become members of the nation but they were members of the Indian state. He maintained that Hindus did not advance any claims, privileges and rights over and above non-Hindu sections. He was ready to concede all rights to the minorities but did not think it necessary to concede the demands of special interests advanced by Muslims.

Thus, Savarkar made a distinction between the Indian state and Hindu nation and considered the Hindu nation as a part of the Indian state.

➢ **Hindu Nationalism of V. D. Savarkar - A Critical Study**

Savarkar was the first Indian thinker who declared that Hindus formed separate nation in, India. He stood for a strong Hindu nation which would withstand and survive ferocious life struggle among the nations. He sought to popularise the Hindu nationalism throughout his life with the help of the Hindu Mahasabha.

There are obvious tensions and logical inconsistencies in the Hindu nationalism of V. D. Savarkar. He could not properly define the concept of nationalism because Hindus, Muslims and Christians shared common traditions and affinities in India even in the religious field. His advocacy of reason, science and technology was instrumental in the sense that for him they were useful because they helped him forge strong Hindu nation. Reason and science in the West were the culmination of the development of social philosophy which fought against religious prejudices and superstitions.

Savarkar's advocacy of the relativist ethics did not resolve these tensions because reason, science and relativist ethics did not recognise ascriptive loyalties. They had to be applied to all human beings across the board.

➢ **The Growth of Hindutva and the Rashtriya Swayam Sevak Sangh (RSS)** IGNOU Book Q.8

The RSS was established by **Dr. Keshav Baliram Hedgewar** in **1925** to protect the interests of the Hindus. Dr. Hedgewar was a follower of Lokmanya Tilak and in his young days, he had contacts with some armed revolutionaries of Calcutta. Hedgewar was close to Dr. B. S. Munje. In

1920-21, Dr. Hedgewar took part in the non-cooperation movement. **Dr. Hedgewar** set *three objectives* before the RSS and they were as follows:
i) Mobilisation of the Hindus to protect their interests and to bring about unity and coherence in all their activities.
ii) Opposition to British militant and communal Muslim politics and the Congress which had been following the policy of appeasement of Muslims.
iii) Increasing the influence of the R.S.S. in all walks of life by patiently undertaking organisational work and by inculcating the spirit of patriotism. According to Dr. Hedgewar, the basic purpose of the RSS was not to capture political power but to increase the influence of Hindus in the public life of the country.

During Dr. Hedgewar's time, the R.S.S. became popular among the white collar middle classes. It did not take part in the civil disobedience movement of 1930 and did not directly get involved in the political activities of the Hindu Mahasabha. In 1940, Dr. Hedgewar nominated a young university Professor Mr. Madhav Golwalkar as the chief of the R.S.S. The RSS did not join the tumultuous Quit India Movement of 1942. Golwalkar continued to occupy the position of the chief of the RSS upto 1973. It was M. S. Golwalkar who expounded the RSS' concept of Hindu natioaalism. His was an impressive personality. He had studied ancient Indian philosophical texts. Throughout his life - Guruji-as he was called, was a great teacher and commanded unique respect and following. His enunciation of the Hindu nationalism became popular among the youth.

HINDU NATIONALISM OF MS GOLWAKAR   IGNOU Book Q.6

The Hindu nationalism of M.S. Golwalkar was different that of V. D. Savarkar in the sense that Golwalkar's theory of nationalism was based on Indian spiritualism. Savarkar was a modernist and he did not oppose westeraisation. But Golwalkar was a supporter of Hindu culture and opposed the Western way of life. He held that the Indian spiritualism was superior to the Western materialism. He believed that India was a holy land and it was the divine will that India should lead the world.

➤ Nation as Motherland

Golwalkar was an exponent of cultural nationalism and he identified nationalism with love for our motherland. He held that the Hindus considered India as their motherland because, since thousands of years they had been identified with this holy land. In this holy land only, Hindus registered all their great achievements. Hindus were children of this ancient land as they were nurtured by water flowing from her rivers and food produced by her rich soil. It was wrong to believe that India became a nation in the recent past.

In fact, she had been existing as a nation since thousands of years. There might be some outward differences, but there existed basic unity in India. All Hindus were bound together by same religion, same language and same culture. The Great Sage Sankara realised this principle and established his religious centres at four different corners of India. He held that all Hindus were permeated by the spirit of unity and solidarity.

GOLWALKAR ON SOCIAL ORGANISATION   IGNOU Book Q.8

M. S. Golwalkar was a supporter of Hindu way of life and looking from that perspective, he found that most of the criticisms levelled against the ancient Indian Varna system were baseless. It was his contention that the present caste system was a degenerated form of the Varna system and the practice of untouchability was inhmman and wrong.

It was his contention that originally, the Varna system was based on the functional specialisation. Charturvarna was considered to be the form of God as the four Varnas constituted his limbs. All Varnas were considered equal and the system was based on mutual help and mutual assistance. All the varnas contributed equally to the growth and prosperity of the society.

Golwalkar was of the opinion that in the Varna system, due to functional specialisation, the people could perfect their skills as a family tradition, avoided competition between the people which was a bane of present capitalist system and ensured sources of livelihood for each and every member of the family. Hence, it was a scheme of employment insurance without the state intervention. Satisfaction of the individual self-discipline and elasticity were the characteristics of the Varna system. Though occasionally, Golwalkar attributed the lack of - unity among the Hindus to caste distinctions, he did not undertake any programme to reform caste system. His justification of the Varna system was a part of the ideological tradition that was developed in modern India in the 19th Century.

POLITICAL IDEAS OF M. S. GOLWALKAR

Galwalkar was of the view that the Indian perspective of nationalism and politics was essentially spiritual, hence, Indians stood for peace and non-violence. But in the changed conditions, Hindus should acquire strength of arms including atom bombs to safeguard their national interests. Hindus faced defeats in the past because they did not acquire latest weapons and militarily they did not prepare themselves well. He agreed with Savarkar that there was a struggle for dominance among different countries of the world; therefore, India should try to become a strong nation.

➢ Three World Views of Change

Golwalkar maintained that capitalism, communism and Hindu spiritualism were three world views of change. He was of the opinion that the Hindu perspective of change was superior to the other two perspectives. According to Golwalkar, the Western models of social organisation and change failed because they laid more stress on the system than on the individual. Infact, Individual was the basis, of the society and hence, development of the individual was the goal of Hindu social life.

➢ Negative and Positive Hindutva   IGNOU Book Q.11

According to Golwalkar, there prevailed two types of Hindutva in India. The first type of Hindutva was called **negative Hindutva** and the second type of Hindutva was called *positive Hindutva*. The negative Hindutva was developed as a reaction to the Muslim communalism or the Congress secularism. The negative Hindutva was based on hatred. It constantly thought negatively about others and vice versa.

Golwalkar was of the opinion that his Hindutva was positive Hindutva in the sense that it was not developed as a reaction to any adversary. It was his contention that the essence of positive Hindutva was the organisation of Hindus as a social force in the society, which would continue to remain steadfast and resolute in the most trying circumstances. The seizure of political power was not the objective of positive Hindutva because it believed that all our problems could not be solved with the help of political power. There were many historical evidences in the past that showed that great empires established with the help of political power were destroyed by the savage invaders. For example, the Roman Empire was reduced to dust by the Huns.

Golwalkar argued that it was the goal of positive Hindutva to remain outside the seat of political power but control it from outside so that it would work in the interest of the society. The greatness of a nation lies not in political power but outside it. Therefore, he pleaded for developing a strong and well organised society which could work as bedrock. He had compared the society to the sun which gave light, energy and strength to the different organs of society. The goal of the RSS was to develop individual as well as society so that it could become strong, united and powerful. The vision of Golwalkar was a political vision and it was based on the programme of an organised and conscious effort to change the social, cultural and political life of the society. Though he rejected political power, the state power as sovereignty and national strength were crucial to his vision of a Hindu nation.

> **Hindu Nationalism of M. S. Golwalkar - A Critical Study**

Along with Savarkar, Golwalkar can be considered as a philosopher of Hindutva. Golwalkar sought to develop his Hindutva on the basis of the Indian spiritualism or non-dualistic monism of Sankaracharya. But there were some tensions in his position because in the "Vedanta", there was unity between the individual soul and the supreme soul. This unity pervaded all human beings including the Hindus and Muslims. The Indian spiritualism did not make distinction between Hindu and non-Hindu souls.

Secondly, he tried to reject the concept of territorial nationalism but his own concept of cultural nationalism was based on territoriality of motherland! His concept of cultural nationalism also faced some problems because his exclusion of Muslims and Christian communities from nation on the grounds of extra-territorial loyalties was questionable. We can give several examples to prove that both Hindu and Muslim communities had produced traitors to nation. The entire community cannot be blamed for the betrayal of a few.

Golwalkar's concept of positive Hindutva, which did not pursue political power, was not convincing because he was a supporter of strong natives and strong nation state. The RSS was not disinterested in political power; perhaps he wanted the RSS to remain outside political power while organisations of the Sangha Parivar could pursue it. The RSS would stand above political power but control it from without. Therefore,

Golwalkar's critique of political power was interesting but difficult to fit into his overall orientation of the militant nationalism.

There were basic differences in the political ideas of Savarkar and Golwalkar. Savarkar's agenda was a modernist agenda and he wanted to establish modern Hindu society in India. He was opposed to both Varna and caste system. He was worshipper of political power and for him state power was crucial in the protection of the country. Golwalkar was opposed to the process of Westernisation and he was of the opinion that negative Hindutva would not be in a position to solve our basic problems. He did not want to abandon the basic principles of the Hindu civilisation; therefore, he supported Varna and caste system.

7.2: IGNOU Book Exercise - Solved

1. Describe briefly causes of emergence of politics of Hindutva in India.

Answer by India Ebook: Read the 1 Shot Concept Above.

2. Write a short note on Savarkar's theory of social change.

Answer by India Ebook: Read the 1 Shot Concept Above.

3. What, according to Savarkar, is the role of social reforms in strengthening the Hindu nation?

Answer by India Ebook: Read the 1 Shot Concept Above.

4. Discuss the main features of Hindu nationalism of V. D. Savarkar.

Answer by India Ebook: Savarkar was the first systematic exponent of the Hindu nationalism. He elaborately described his theory of Hindutva in his book 'Hindutva' published in 1924. In the process of developing his concept of Hindu nationalism, he rejected some of the arguments of territorial nationalism. He held that the existence of a mere territory did not make nation but nation was made by the people who constituted themselves as a political community, bound together by cultural affinities and traditions.

Savarkar was a supporter of cultural nationalism. He was of the opinion that identity formation was the essence of nationalism. India had received such identity from the Hindu religion. This identity was evolved over a long period of time. Despite having outward differences, the Hindus were internally bound together by cultural, religious, social, linguistic and historical affinities.

Savarkar argued that it was cultural, racial and religious unity that counted more in the formation of the nation. While defining nation, Savarkar wrote that nation meant a political community which had occupied a contiguous and adequate territory and developed independent national identity. This community was internally organised and was bound together by cultural and racial affinities. He held that the Hindus had become nation because they possessed all these characteristics.

Savarkar was of the opinion that Hindus constituted nation because they had developed close affinities with the land bound by Himalayas to the Indian Ocean and the Indus River. Hindus considered India as their fatherland and holy land. Savarkar tried to show that those people constituted nation who considered India as fatherland and holy land. In this definition, Savarkar effectively excluded those people wlio did not consider India as their holy land - because their sacred religious places were not situated in India. For him, Hindu nationalism stood for the unity of all Hindus.

5. Bring out Savarkar's views on nation and state.

Answer by India Ebook: Read the 1 Shot Concept Above.

6. Examine briefly Golwalkar's ideas on Hindu nationalism.

Answer by India Ebook: Read the 1 Shot Concept Above.

7. Why does Golwalkar support the Hindu social organisation? Give reasons.

Answer by India Ebook: Read the 1 Shot Concept Above.

8. Write a short note on the rise of the RSS in Indian politics.

Answer by India Ebook: Read the 1 Shot Concept Above.

9. **Critically** examine Golwalkar's ideas on Hindu nationalism.

Answer by India Ebook: Read the 1 Shot Concept Above.

10. What advice did Golwalkar give to the religious minorities in India?

Answer by India Ebook: Golwalkar rejected the concept of the Indian or territorial nationalism as reality. He claimed that due to certain historical and cultural factors, Hindus in India constituted a nation and they considered India as their motherland. Though most of the converted Muslims and Christians were originally Hindus, because of their conversion, they lost their devotion and affection for motherland. They started claiming the foreign racial genealogies as their own. Therefore,

Golwalkar was of the opinion that these minorities could not be considered as a part of the Hindu nation.

Golwalkar was of the opinion that the non-Hindu minorities could also become a part of the Indian nation, if they abandoned their separatist tendencies and accepted all the traditions as their own. He exhorted the Muslims and the Christians to join the mainstream and be a part of the Hindu national tradition. He held that these communities should Indianise themselves by accepting and imbibing the Hindu cultural and historical traditions. They should consider themselves as inheritors of the great Hindu heroes described in the epics and take part in the celebration of Hindu festivals. They should imbibe the Hindu way of life.

He pointed out that it was not necessary for them to leave their religion. They should practice their religion as they wanted because they had freedom of religion and worship. Also, by accepting the Hindu way of life, they could remain Muslims and Christians. It was high time that they should return back to home and be a part of the great national tradition. Golwalkar said that he did not want to do this with the help of coercion or force, but through love and persuasion. He held that the minorities would enjoy all social and political rights but they would not be given any privileges.

11. Discuss Golwalkar's views on positive Hindutva.

Answer by India Ebook: Read the 1 Shot Concept Above.

7.3: IGNOU Past 6 Attempts Question – Solved

June 2021: Describe the salient features of M.S. Golwalkar's Hindu Nationalism.

Answer by India Ebook: Same as Q.6 and Q.9 of Above.

June 2020: Elaborate M.S. Golwalkar's vision of negative and positive Hindutava.

Answer by India Ebook: Same as Q.11 of Above.

June 2019: Write an essay on Hindu Nationalism of V.D. Savarkar.

Answer by India Ebook: Same as Q.4 of Above.

Dec 2018: Analyse V.D. Savarkar's views on nation and state.

Answer by India Ebook: Same as Q.5 of Above.

8. MUSLIM THOUGHT: SIR SYED AHMED KHAN, MOHAMMED IQBAL, MAULANA MAUDOODI AND MOHAMMED ALI JINNAH

Introduction

Sir Syed Ahmed Khan (1817- 1898)
- ➢ Contribution to Modern Education
- ➢ Hindu Muslim Unity

Mohammed Iqbal (1876-1938)
- ➢ Early Life
- ➢ Ideas on Nationalism
- ➢ Political Activities

Maulana Maudoodi (1903-1979)
- ➢ Views on Nationalism

Mohammed Ali Jinnah (1876- 1948)
- ➢ Hindu-Muslim Unity
- ➢ Jinnah and the Muslim League
- ➢ Two Nation Theory

8.1: One Shot Concepts

INTRODUCTION

The Muslim thought in modern India can be understood properly only in its larger historical setting. It is important to note that the evolution of the Muslim political thought was a complex phenomenon involving historical context of the Muslims social, cultural and political life and interactive process with the colonial rule which had been established in India particularly in the aftermath of the Revolt of 1857.

Several issues had emerged, such as relative backwardness of Muslims in relations to modern tendencies which had come in the wake of the establishment of the colonial rule. The question of accommodation of various social groups including Muslims in the existing and future power structures became an important issue which was widely debated among all groups. Equally important was the issue of religio-cultural identity of various communities which went through a process of redefinition in the late 19th century as well as the first half of the 20th century. All these issues emerged over the years with varying responses from different social groups which, in the long run, affected inter-community relations. These developments also affected the political processes which were unfolding in the course of an articulation of anti-colonial nationalist ideology.

SIR SYED AHMAD KHAN (1817-1898)

Sir Syed Ahmad Khan was one of the most formidable figures of the late 19th century India. He emerged on the Indian scene as one of the great reformers, educationist and moderniser within the Muslim community. He was born on 17th October 1817 in one of the respected families associated with the Mughal court. Sir Syed was a direct witness to the declining fortunes of the Mughals and was conscious about the fact that while the glory of the Mughals was as good as gone, the political force which was gaining ground was that of the British.

Sir Syed, having seen the Revolt and subsequently its brutal suppression by the British, was convinced that the British were too powerful and any attempt to resist them might not be fruitful at all. From this time onwards, the British started suspecting the Muslims at large as they were violently opposed to them (British). As a consequence of such an approach, the Muslims were treated more harshly than any other social group involved in the Revolt.

➤ Contribution to Modern Education

Sir Syed was, by now, convinced that in order to stem the declining fortunes of the Muslims, it was important that they took to modern education as it was introduced by the British. With this purpose in mind, he founded the Scientific Society in 1863 at Ghazipur, in Uttar Pradesh. The basic objective was to translate scientific literature, into Urdu. In this project, he was supported by all including several Hindu friends, The subjects such as mechanics, electricity, pneumatics and natural philosophy received particular emphasis. Subsequetly, this society was shifted to Aligarh. In 1866, Sir Syed started a journal on behalf of the Society called the Indian Institute Gazette.

During 1869-70, he travelled to England and was able to observe the British educational institutions and was impressed by them. Upon his return from this extended journey he developed an idea that in order to improve educational standards of the Muslims of India, there must be modern educational institutions for them. This was the larger objective in mind with which he founded Mohammedan Anglo-Oriental (MAO) College in 1875/ 1877. It was proposed that here, while modern education would be imparted to the Muslims, they would abo have some training in the preservation of their cultural heritage. It is interesting to note that while MAO College was founded for Muslims, its doors were open to all.

➤ Hindu-Muslim Unity   IGNOU Book Q.1

Sir Syed was also a champion of the Hindu-Muslim unity. He had once described the Hindus and Muslims as two beautiful eyes of a beautiful bride. He wrote two essays in Tahzib-ul-Akhlaq, one in 1888 and another 1898 exhorting Muslims to give up killing of cows since this would bring about a good neighbourly relations between the Hindus and the Muslims. There were innumerable occasions when he strongly advocated for this unity between the two important religious communities.

While these were some aspects of the various thoughts of Sir Syed where he was committed to larger well being of the Muslims, there were certain other aspects as well where he seemed to suggest distinct political options for the Muslims and did not wish them ever to come closer to the Congress. Some of these tendencies were visible from the time the movement to replace Urdu in Persian script with that of Hindi in Nagari script had emerged in the United Provinces in 1867. The protagonist of this movement had argued that Urdu was not the language of the masses as Hindi was, and thus, such a demand was raised.

Sir Syed maintained that these communities would have distinct political options separate from each other. This was the driving force which made him argue that the Indian National Congress was not in the best interest of the community of Muslims. Sir Syed was also opposed to the principle of election even for the local boards and district boards. He argued that keeping in view the minds of social differences that existed in the Indian society, it would be imprudent to introduce the principle of elections.

It is important to remember that in a country such as India where diversity of all hues existed for such a long time, religious communities were no exception. Every community threw up diverse options keeping in mind the class, linguistic, regional and other backgrounds in mind.

After all Sir Syed was not preaching any hatred between communities. However his major concerns were to promote the interests of the Muslims at large particularly the established groups. Sir Syed Ahmad Khan died on 27th March 1898.

MOHAMMAD IQBAL (1876-1938)

Mohammad Iqbal is commonly referred to as Allama Iqbal for the reason that he was considered as one of the important intellectuals among the Muslims in the first half of the 20th century. He started his career as a poet rather early in life who, later on, acquired immense maturity. He is one of the few Urdu poets whose compositions required prior initiation for better comprehension.

> ### Early Life

Mohaminad Iqbal was born on 22nd February 1873 at Sialkot, in Punjab. His forefathers were Kashmiri Brahmins who had embraced Islam about three hundred years ago. Mohammad Iqbal looked at his ancestry with pride and gave enough reflection to it in his poetry as well. His initial education was in a traditional Maktab. Later he joined Sialkot Mission School and upon completing matriculation, he went to Lahore for higher studies and joined the Government College there and completed his B.A. in 1897.

Two years later, he secured his Masters' degree and was appointed as a lecturer in the Oriental College, Lahore to teach History, Philosophy and English where he served between 1899 and 1905. He went to Europe and secured a Ph.D at Munich and returned to Lahore in 1908. In the course of his stay in Europe, he also obtained degree to practice as a barrister.

> ### Ideas on Nationalism IGNOU Book Q.2

Before Mohammad Iqbal had visited Europe he was given to espouse a rather strong sense of patriotism. For instance his famous song *Sare Jahan se Achcha Hindustan Humara* was the ultimate tribute to the motherland, India. His poem, **Naya Shivala** too was an example of sincere exhortations to his countrymen to give up pettymindedness and develop broader vision and perspective about the corporate life as Indians.

However, upon his return from Europe he seemed to develop some distaste for nationalism because of the way various European nations were pursuing this, The period he was in Europe was truly an age of aggressive nationalism. Nations were attempting to run down each other. Such observations of Iqbal led him to believe that nationalism was too narrow an ideology to make an ideal of human & territorial groups.

However, the point that must be noted here is that nationalism in a colonial society such as India was not directed towards dominating any other nation but seek liberation from colonial rule and exploitation at the hands of the British. The Indian nationalism, as it was unfolding in the course of its evolution, was more progressive than jingoistic.

➢ Political Activities

While Iqbal had his one step firmly rooted in poetry and philosophy, his second step gradually started setting into the world of politics as well. He had become familiar with the Muslim League propagation of the demand for separate electorates while he was still in England in 1906. After his return to India in 1908, he joined the provincial Muslim League in Punjab. From this time onwards, Iqbal's concerns remained only with the promotion of the Muslims' interests.

In order to engage himself in this exercise, he argued with Muslims that there was no point in opposing the British. He disagreed with many Muslim individuals and groups who were active in the freedom struggle and accused them of harbouring too much of the Western ideas which he thought the nationalism were.

Iqbal was elected to the Punjab Legislative Asselnbly in 1927 and actively participated in the debates of the Assembly. While participating in the Budget discussion on 5th March 1927, he pleaded for more allocation for rural sanitation and medical relief for women. In the course of the proceedings of the House, he also pleaded for more funds for mass education, which he thought was absolutely essential in the interest of the people.

In the wake of the communal riots in Punjab in 1927, he pleaded for harmony among the communities. While Iqbal was a member of the Punjab Legislative Assembly he was elected the Secretary of All Indian Muslim League. But he soon ran into differences with many leaders of the League on the the issue of the boycott of Simon Commission, which was an all white commission for making suggesstions to bring constitutional changes in the existing Government India Act 1919. He left the Secretalyship of the League but continued to remain loyal to the ideology and larger principles of the party. Later in 1930 he was invited to preside over the session of the Muslim League at Allahabad. In this session he delivered a speech which was to have delineated certain options which hitherto was not envisaged by anybody else.

However, it has to be noted that Iqbal did not maintain consistency in his formulations on the question of nationalism. In March 1933 he remarked that nationalism implied certain race consciousness which was against the grain of his conviction. Iqbal's participation in the contemporary political process was full of contradiction and inconsistencies. However his contributions in the realm of poetic creativity were far more enduring. He breathed his last on 21st April 1938.

MWULANA MAUDUDI (1903-1979)

Syed Abul A'la Maududi popularly known as Maulana Maududi, is one of the greatest revivalists of Islam in the 20th century. Apart from having produced a large number of literature concerning Islam and Muslims, he was the founder of the *Jamat-i-Islami* in 1941. Maulana Maududi was born on **2nd September 1903** in a devout Muslim family of Aurangabad, in the present day Maharashtra. His educational training was steeped in Islamic studies right from the beginning. Towards the close of the second decade of the 20th century he was drawn to the nationalist movement in the wake of the Non-cooperation-Khilafat movement and was impressed by Gandhiji's work so much that he wrote a book on his persollality and work but it was confiscated by the British Government.

He became the editor of the paper launched by it called the Muslim and served it till the end of 1923 when this paper was closed. Subsequently the *Jamiat-ul-Ulema-i-Hind* launched another paper called *al-Jamiat* which Maulana Maududi again joined it as the editor and continued to serve the paper till the end of 1927.

However Maulana Maududi did not have any defined pursuit of career. He came to much wider prominence with the editorship of *Tarjzmman-ul-Quran* at Hyderabad since 1936. His writings attracted even Mohammad Iqbal, who invited him to **Pathankot** and pursue his studies there. He offered the support of some **Wakf** property there. He moved to Pathankot in January 1938 to establish Darul Islam Academy. However the death of Mohammad Iqbal soon after, made Maulana Maududi return to Lahore to teach Islamiyat at Islamia College there.

MOHAMMAD ALI JINNAH (1876-1948)

Mohammad Ali Jinnah travelled long distances in his political career finally to become the Qaid-i-Azam, which literally means a great leader to the Pakistanis since he had the credit of founding Pakistan after seeking the partition of India on 14th August 1947. Mohatnmad Ali Jinnah was born on 2Sth December 1976 in the family of a relatively prosperous business family of Jinnabhai in Karachi. After his initial education in Karachi and Bombay, Jinnah went to England to study law which he soon completed at the age of 18 years with two more years of stay there at Lincoln Inn's formal training. At the age of twenty he returned to India to join the Bar first in Karachi and later in Bombay and soon established himself among the legal fraternity of the city.

Jinnah became a part of the Congress led politics by joining the party in 1906. At the annual session of the Congress, the same year, he acted as the private secretary to Dadabhai Nauroji who was the president of the Indian National Congress for that year. He came quite close to a moderate Congress leader, Gopal Krishna Gokhale and received his initial political training under him and soon earned recognition. He was a part of the battery of lawyers who defended Lokmanya Tilak in 1908 when he was prosecuted by the British.

Jinnah supported Gokhale in 1912 when he came up with the Elementary Education Bill and argued for more allocation of money for the purpose. While Jinnah was still in the Congress, he joined the Muslim League as well on the suggestion of Maulana Mohammad Ali and Wazir Husain in 1913. However before joining the League, he ensured that joining it never meant any compromise on the larger national cause as espoused by the Congress. The same year he was instrumental in accepting the Wakf Validating Bill by the then Viceroy, which was meant to safeguard the interests of the beneficiaries of the Muslim family trusts against the folly of any one member of the family. This particular act of Jinnah earned him recognition among the Muslims.

8.2: IGNOU Book Exercise – Solved

1. Analyse Sir Syed Ahmad Khan's views on Hindu-Muslim Unity.
Answer by India Ebook: Read the 1 Shot Concept Above.

2. Summarise Mohammad Iqbal's ideas on Nationalism and his contribution to the Muslim Thought.
Answer by India Ebook: Read the 1 Shot Concept Above.

3. The Islamic nationhood and geographical nationalism, as Maulana Maududi argued, are two distinct identities. Explain.
Answer by India Ebook: Syed Abul A'la Maududi popularly known as Maulana Maududi, is one of the greatest revivalists of Islam in the 20th century. Apart from having produced a large number of literature concerning Islam and Muslims, he was the founder of the *Jamat-i-Islami* in 1941. Maulana Maududi was born on **2nd September 1903** in a

devout Muslim family of Aurangabad, in the present day Maharashtra. His educational training was steeped in Islamic studies right from the beginning. Towards the close of the second decade of the 20th century he was drawn to the nationalist movement in the wake of the **Non-cooperation-Khilafat** movement and was impressed by Gandhiji's work so much that he wrote a book on his persollality and work but it was confiscated by the British Government.

In Maududi's perception, Islamic and geographical nationalism were two mutually exclusive entities, therefore he was apprehensive that geographical nationalism among Muslims would undermine Islamic 'nationhood' and unity. He thought that Indian leaders were mistaken in their belief that in order to fight the British, they must create a common nationality. He disagreed with Husain Ahmad Madani's contention that in the Indian context a religious community did not constitute a nation unto itself.

On the contrary, ail religious communities must politically merge together in order to emerge as a distinct nation on territorial basis. However while Husain Ahmad Madani was making these arguments on behalf of the Jamiatul-Ulema-i-Hind, he was also conscious of the fact that while Muslims were willing to join the process of the making of a nation, they must retain their distinct religio-cultural identity. Maududi's notion of Islamic 'nationality' reached an incomprehensible length when he argued that all those who were struggling against the British should be aware that if the British were to transfer power to non-Muslims then the very participation of a Muslim in this process would not be valid from the point of view of religion.

4. Briefly analyse M.A. Jinnah's contribution to the 'Two Nation Theory'.

Answer by India Ebook: In its opposition to the Congress, the Muslim League crossed all limits and finally came around to the idea of describing the Muslims of India not as a religious community or a minority in a Hindu-majority country but a distinct nation. Thus according to the League's formulations, India was home to not one but two nations which led the demand that India be partitioned so that there could be separate homeland to the Muslims as well. This understanding was put to crystallisation in the **annual session** of the Muslim League held in **Lahore** on 23rd March 1940.

The Resolution adopted here is popularly known as the **Pakistan Resolution** or 'Two-nation theory'. In this resolution it was said that the Muslims of India on account of their religious, cultural and historical distinctiveness in contrast with the Hindus, constituted a nation unto themselves. Since then, Jinnah reiterated this position on all occasions and from all platforms. From this time onwards, the Muslim League, under Jinnah, did not look back and never considered any settlement which was not conceding Pakistan.

In this effort of the League, the British Government was more than obliging right since the time of **August offer** of **1940** and right through the *Cripps Mission* of *1942* and the **Cabinet Mission** of **1946**. In the Simla Conference held in 1945, Jinnah had argued that in the event of any interim arrangements of ministry formation, only the Muslim League would have the right to nominate Muslim members. In an unsaid manner, Lord Wavel, the then Viceroy, conceded this demand raised by the Muslim League.

As a consequence many Muslim political leaders in provinces such as Punjab switched sides in favour of the League and in the elections of 1945-46 it was able to secure almost 75% of the Muslim votes. However it is important to mention that these elections were held under the provisions of the **Government of India Act 1935** and the average franchised percentage did not exceed more than 15% of the total population, Muslims being no exception to it.

8.3: IGNOU Past 6 Attempts Question - Solved

Dec 2021: Examine M.A. Jinnah's contribution towards Muslim nationalism.

June 2020: Assess the changes in M.A. Jinnaha's views on Muslim Nationalism.

June 2019: Examine M.A. Jinnah's role in development of Muslim Nationalism.

Answer by India Ebook: Refer 1 Shot Concept Above for all 3 Questions

Dec 2018: Describe Sir Syed Ahmad Khan's views on Hindu - Muslim unity.

Answer by India Ebook: Same as Q.1 of Above.

9. NATION & IDENTITY CONCERNS: EV RAMASWAMY NAICKER, NAZRUL ISLAM, PANDITA RAMABAI, JAIPAL SINGH, KHAN SINGH

Introduction

E. V. Ramaswamy Naicker (1879-1973)

- o Critique of Hinduism and Brahminical Domination
- o Critique of the Congress and Mahatma Gandhi
- o Naicker's Discourse
- o Dravidian Mobilisation

Pandita Ramabai (1858-1922)

- o Early Life: Non-conformist Background
- o Contesting Patriarchy: Hinduism and Christianity

Jaipal Singh (1903-1970)

- o Championing Adivasi Identity

Kazi Nazrul Islam (1899-1976)

- o The Rebel Poet (Bidhrohi Kobi)
- o Hindu-Muslim Issue

Bhai Kahn Singh Nabha (1861-1938)

- o Hum Hindu Nahin: We are not Hindus

9.1: One Shot Concepts

INTRODUCTION

Concern for Indian nation was never expressed in a homogeneous way. Social and political thinkers of modern India understood the nature of Indian society and polity in different ways for obvious reasons; therefore, construction of nation was never uniforM. While some of them designed an overarching and encompassing Indian identity, others constructed Indian nation on the foundation of particular identities like religion, caste, ethnicity and gender, language, etc.

E. V. RAMASWAMY NAICKER (1879-1973)

E.V. Ramaswamy Naicker, popularly known as Periyar (Great Sage), was born in Erode, in a family of well-off artisans. He married at an early age of 13, but after six years became an ascetic. Wandering all over

India, particularly the Hindu pilgrimage centres, he experienced the 'evils' of Hinduism and the priestly exploitations.

➢ Critique of Hinduism and Brahminical Domination

Periyar's negative perception of Hinduism and Brahmins needs to be analysed in the socio-political context of Tamil Nadu. Like their counterparts in other provinces, in Tamil Nadu as well, Brahmins always enjoyed a dominant position in the Hindu scriptures and rituals. Though constituted only about 3 per cent of Tamils, they continued to dominate the public spheres even under the colonial rule. Their settlement in fertile areas further enhanced their social power. In the pre-colonial Tamil Nadu, although Brahmins did not monopolise the ownership of land, they virtually monopolised scribal occupation, which enabled them to acquire Western education much faster than others under the colonial rule. This gave the Brahmins an early lead in the professions.

To Naicker, Hinduism was a tool of Brahminical domination and the Brahmins epitomised Hindu arrogance and perpetrated social injustice. He castigated Hinduism as an opiate by which the Brahmins had dulled and subdued the masses. Naicker was convinced that Hinduism perpetuated casteism, and must be resisted. Thus, he publicly ridiculed the Puranas as fairy tales, not only imaginary and irrational but also grossly immoral.

➢ Critique of the Congress and Mahatma Gandhi

The scope of the associational activity and self-government increased in the early decades of the century. Brahmins set the tone of Madras city politics in the 1910s, of the Home Rule Leagues sprouting during the World War I and of nationalist mobilisation after the War. They controlled Congress's state level leadership until World War II, Naicker was active in the Congress-led Freedom Struggle for sometime. He participated in the non-cooperation movement, offered satyagraha and defended khadi. But Naicker's efforts to get Tamil Nadu Congress to adopt resolutions in favour of caste quotas in political representation were continually defeated between 1919 and 1925.

Periyar was opposed to Gandhi's reconstructed version of varnashrama dharma as it did not correspond to the way the caste system had historically functioned. Periyar also interpreted Gandhian nationalism as a hegemonic project to maintain the dominance of the Brahmins and 'Brahminism' in Indian society and the predominant influence of north India in the national politics. Naicker's growing dissatisfaction with Gandhi and the Congress, which he began to express from 1925 onwards in the journal Kudi Arasu, led him and his followers to found the Self Respect Association in 1926.

Protesting against the Brahminical dominance in high politics, he quit the Congress and developed Dravidian cultural alternatives to the prevailing hegemonic Brahminical culture. In 1925, he organised the "Self Respect Movement", designed as Dravidian Uplift, seeking to expose Brahminical tyranny and the deceptive methods by which they controlled all spheres of Hindu life.

➢ Naicker's Discourse

Portraying Naicker as just anti-Brahmin or anti-God would be not doing justice. He was a radical social reformer. His determined campaign against Hindu orthodoxy accompanied by rationalism and social reform, transformed the social landscape of Tamil Nadu. His radical social reform campaign caught the imagination of the underclass: As in the Self-Respect Movement, one of Naicker's basic objectives was to remove all "superstitious belief' based upon religion or tradition. No member was allowed to wear the sectarian marks of faith across his forehead. Members were urged to boycott the use of Brahmin priests in ceremonies. He campaigned for widow remarriage and inter-caste marriage. Thus, his thrust on non-Brahminism must be placed in the context of the rigid rituals that had legitimised caste oppression at that time.

Naicker claimed that his brand of politics was oriented on the contrary, towards the emancipation of the subordinate groups in Tamil society, much as fiberalism had opposed upper class and clerical dominance in the West. Naicker sought to associate himself with the enlightenment heritage by elaborating a materialist ontology and a genealogy of Brahminical morals as founded on a resentment of worldly non-Brahmin virtues.

Important aspects of Naicker's ideology and the manner in which it was deployed in mobilisation were out of tune with liberalism. Far from relying on the concept of abstract citizen central to British liberalism, Naicker adopted ethnic categories drawn from colonial knowledge and sought to accord Shudra primacy in the political community. Thus, the emancipatory potential of Naicker's notions of social identity remained a subsidiary aspect of dravidianist project right through.

> **Dravidian Mobilisation**   IGNOU Book Q.1 & 2

Naicker conceived Dravidian community primarily in terms of a coalition of megacastes the non-Brahmin Hindu castes of Tamil Nadu, i.e. Tamil speaking Hindus who were neither Brahmins nor SCs. Non-Brahminism endured in Tamil Nadu because it was linked to Tamil nationalism from the 1930s onwards in a populist discourse. The opposition to Brahmin dominance had the potential of serving as a banner for subordinate non-Brahmin groups to buttress their dominance.

Under the Congress Ministry of C. Rajagopalachari in 1937, Hindi was introduced to the South as a compulsory subject in schools. Taking it as an affront to Tamil culture and its rich literary traditions, Naicker waved black flags of rebellion in his first anti-Hindi campaign. The campaign forced the government to change Hindi into an optional subject. Naicker saw the imposition of Hindi as a subjugation of Tamil people which could be avoided only through the creation of a Dravidian state. In 1938, Naicker was elected President of the Justice Party.

In 1939, Naicker organised the "Dravida Nadu Conference" for the advocacy of a separate and independent Dravidasthan. The demand was again reiterated the following year in response to the Lahore resolution demanding Pakistan passed by the Muslim League. Naicker gave full support to the scheme for Pakistan and tried to enlist support for the creation of a Dravidasthan. The basic presupposition of the movement was that the Dravidian non-Brahmin peoples (Tamil, Telugu, Kannada, and Malayalam) were of a racial stock and culture, which distinguished them from the Aryan Brahmins.

In 1944, the justice Party was reorganised as Dravida Kazagham(DK). The object of the DK was proclaimed to be the attainment of a sovereign independent Republic, which would be federal in nature with four units corresponding to the linguistic divisions, each having residual powers and autonomy of internal administration.

PANDITA RAMABAI (1858-1922)   IGNOU Book Q.3

Pandita Ramabai (1858-1922) was one of the greatest **women of modern India**. Exceptionally learned, Ramabai, an outspoken champion of women's rights and social reform, earned the unique distinction of being the *sole woman representative* in the male-dominated world of gender reforms. As Ramabai 'transgressed' the boundaries and contested patriarchy in her educational and missionary activities, she understandably became the most controversial uppercaste woman of her times, and hence, was consciously 'erased' from the modern Indian history for a long period.

➤ Early Life: Non-conformist Background

Ramabai's father Anant Shastri Dongre, a Chitpavan Brahmin, a non-conformist, invited the era of his powerful conservative community brethren when he decided to teach Sanskrit to his wife which was regarded 'heretical. Sanskrit, the 'divine language' was after all reserved for the uppercaste men.

Ramabai learnt Sanskrit and Puranas in those hard days, full of suffering and pain. Thus, Ramabai's break with Brahminism was inevitable, considering the life and the legacy she inherited from her father. After the death of her parents, Ramabai arrived in Calcutta in 1878 at the age of nineteen. Interestingly, the religious elite of the city warmly welcomed her and encouraged her to study the Vedas and Upanishads despite the prohibition on women to do so. She impressed the religious elite of the city with her mastery over Sanskrit language and texts and received the title of 'Pandita' (Scholar) and 'Saraswati' (Goddess of Learning). Ramabai soon took up her social reform agenda by travelling widely in Bengal and addressing women on the need for their education and emancipation, drawing heavily on the mythological figures of educated and independent women.

JAIPAL SINGH (1903-1970)   IGNOU Book Q.4

Jaipal Singh (1903-1970), was a multi-faceted personality-a distinguished parliamentarian, a champion sportsman, an educationist, a powerful orator and above all, the leader of the Adivasis. Jaipal alias Pramod Pahan was born at the Takra village of Khunti subdivision of the present day Jharkhand. In childhood, his job was to look after the cattle herd. His destiny had a turn around with his admission to St. Paul's School, Ranchi, in 1910. Then Jaipal moved to England and graduated from St John's College, Oxford with Honours in Economics.

Jaipal was selected in Indian Civil Service from which he later resigned. In 1928 Amsterdam Olympics, he captained the Indian hockey team which won the gold medal. In 1934, Jaipal joined teaching at the Prince of Wales College at Achimota, Gold Coast, Ghana. In 1937, he returned to India as the principal incumbent of the Rajkumar College, Raipur. In 1938, he joined the Bikaner princely State as foreign secretary. Jaipal thought that with his varied experience he could be more useful to the country through the Congress. His encounter with Rajendra Prasad at the Sadaaquat Ashram in Patna, however, did not go well. The then Governor of Bihar, Sir Maurice Hallet offered to nominate him to the Bihar Legislative Council but Jaipal declined. In deference to their wishes, Jaipal then decided to go to Ranchi and assess the situation for himself. The return to Ranchi was Jaipal's homecoming.

When the news got around that Jaipal had arrived in Ranchi, there was great excitement among the Adivasis. The united Adivasi forum called Adivasi Sabha, formed in 1938 made him the president of the-organisation. As many as 65,000 people gathered to listen to Jaipal's presidential speech on January 20, 1939. They came from all over, walked on foot for days together to have a glimpse of him as they had done in the past for Birsa Munda, the legend. His oratory, simultaneously in English, Hindi, Sadani and Mundari, mesmerised men and women from all walks of life.

KAZI NAZRUL ISLAM (1899-1976)   IGNOU Book Q.5

Kazi Nazrul Islam (1899-1976), the national poet of Bangladesh, was born in Churulia, Burdharnan district, West Bengal. He lost his father in his childhood and had a financial hardship, thereby forced to work as a teacher in a lower Islamic school at the age of nine. Though his education went only up to tenth grade, he continued learning Arabic and Persian languages. As a boy, he translated Persian ghazals and Arabic writings in Bengali. He also educated himself enough to enjoy the writings of Keats, Shelly and Whitman. Nazrul became a literary genius, writing 50 books of poetry and songs, 6 books of stories and novels, 3 books of translations, 53 plays, verse-plays and operas, 2 movie scripts, 5 books of essays and 4000 songs and ghazals. He holds the world record of recorded songs, for most of which, the music was composed by Nazrul himself.

> The Rebel Poet (Bidhrohi Kobi)

Nazrul was opposed to the British rule of India and took an active part through his writings on Swadishi and Khilafat movement. He had to undergo rigorous imprisonment for a year for his writing Andamoyeer Agamaney which appeared in Dhumketu. Rabindranath Tagore called Nazrul "Dhumketu" - the Comet. For Mahatma Gandhi, Nazrul's poem was "the song of thew spinning wheel" and Nazrul was "the ultimate spirit of the spinning wheel" and freedom ran through his vein.

Nazrul same to be known as Bidrohi Kobi-the rebel poet-for his astonishing masterpiece "The Bidrohi." This was a furious manifesto of self-conscious against immoraljty. It is said that Nazrul would have been Nazrul even if he had not written anything else but "The Bidrohi." Thus, Kazi Nazrul Islam refused to compromise with the unjust.

BHAI KAHN SINOH NABHA (1861-1938)　　IGNOU Book Q.6

Bhai Kahn Singh, a distinguished Sikh scholar, was born in the village of Sabaz Banera, Patiala. His father Narain Singh was the in-charge of a Gurdwara at Nabha. Kahn Singh did not attend any formal school or college, yet he mastered several branches of learning through traditional education. By the age of ten he could recite with ease the Guru Granth Sahib. He also studied Sanskrit as well as Persian. In 1887, he was appointed tutor to Tikka Ripudaman Singh, the heir apparent of Sikh State of Nabha. From the Maharaja's private secretary to the judge of the High Court, he held different positions in the state.

In 1885, he accidentally met Max Arthur Macauliffe who was working on Sikh scriptures and history of early Sikhism. Macauliffe took Kahn Singh to England and depended a great deal on his advice and guidance acknowledging his contribution; he assigned Kahn Singh the copyright of his 6-volume The Sikh Religion.

> **Hum Hindu Nahin: We are not Hindus**

In 1898, he published Hum Hindu Nahin (We are not Hindus) with a specific purpose. The title makes Kahn Singh's view abundantly dear. It was a response to the Arya Samaj propaganda that Sikhs were just a sect of Hindus. His book set forth forcefully the Sikh standpoint with regard to the Sikh identity. It represented the dominant view of the Singh Sabha movement and has ever since retained the fame, which it so quietly acquired. It is worth stressing that the approach adopted in this book is neither hostile nor aggressive. In his presentation, he took great care to stress that he sought peace, not discord.

9.2: IGNOU Book Exercise – Solved

1) Explain Naicker's ideology of mobilisation to establish just serial order.
Answer by India Ebook: Read the 1 Shot Concept Above.

2) Write a note on Naicker's Dravidian of movement in Tamil Nadu.
Answer by India Ebook: Read the 1 Shot Concept Above.

3) Explain pandita Rama Bai's contribution to Women's rise and reform.
Answer by India Ebook: Read the 1 Shot Concept Above.

4) Write a note on Jaipal Singh's political leadership.
Answer by India Ebook: Read the 1 Shot Concept Above.

5) Explain the various contribution of Nazrul Islam to the growth of Nationalism in India.
Answer by India Ebook: Read the 1 Shot Concept Above.

6) Write a note on Bhai Kahn Singh and his views on Sikh identity.
Answer by India Ebook: Read the 1 Shot Concept Above.

9.3: IGNOU Past 6 Attempts Question – Solved

June 2021: Discuss E.V. Ramaswamy Naicker's critique of Hinduism and Brahmanical Domination.
Answer by India Ebook: Refer 1 Shot Concept Above.
June 2020: Discuss E.V. Ramaswamy Naicker's role in Dravidian mobilisation.
Answer by India Ebook: Same as Q.2 of Above.
Dec 2020: Discuss Pandita Rama Bai's role towards women's empowerment.
Answer by India Ebook: Same as Q.3 of Above.
June 2019: Critically evaluate E.V. Ramaswamy, Naicker's contribution to Darvidian movement.
Answer by India Ebook: Refer 1 Shot Concept Above.
Dec 2018: Discuss E.V. Ramaswamy Naicker's critique of Hinduism.
Answer by India Ebook: Refer 1 Shot Concept Above.

10. M. K. GANDHI

Introduction
Philosophical Foundations of Gandhi's Political Perspective
Views on Human Nature
Relationship between Religion and Politics
> Concept of Religion
> Concept of Politics
> Relationship between Religion and Politics
Unity of Ends and Means
> Relationship Between Means and Ends
Satya, Satyagraha and Ahimsa
Concept of Swaraj
On Parliamentary Democracy
Grain Swaraj or Development from Below
Ideas on the Economy
Sarvodaya: The Rise of All
Theory of Trusteeship
Evils of Industrialism
Concept of Swadeshi

10.1: One Shot Concepts

INTRODUCTION

Mohandas Karamchand Gandhi (1869-1948), herein after Gandhiji, was undoubtedly the most authentic and celebrated representative of the wisdom and culture of India in our times. His countrymen address him, with respect, as the Mahatma. For Many, among the greatest, Gandhiji was the great. He was a social reformer, an economist, a political philosopher and a seeker of truth. We consider him as a 'yugapurusha', one who inaugurated a new era.

The contribution of Mohandas Karamchand Gandhi to the Indian national movement was unparalleled. He made the Indian National Congress a peoples' Congress and the national movement a mass movement. He made people fearless and bold and taught them the non-violent methods for fighting against injustice. He had a passion for individual liberty which was closely bound with his understanding of truth and self-realisation.

A spiritual perspective infuses Gandhiji's whole approach to life. His political understanding and practices, suggestions on the economy, social mobilisation and practical life have their basis in morality and ethics.

Pursuit of Truth is his mantra and non-violence was integral to it. Among Gandliiji's notable writings, mention may be made of An Autobiography: The Story, of my Experiments with Truth; The Collected Works of Mahatma Gandhi; Panchayati Raj; Satyagraha in South Africa; Sarvodaya and Hind Swaraj. He edited Young India which he later renanied as Harijnn which remained his mouthpiece.

PHILOSOPHICAL FOUNDATIONS OF GANDHI'S POLITICAL PERSPECTIVE   IGNOU Book Q.1

Gandhiji was a deeply religious man.This perspective shaped his politics, his economic ideas and his view of society. However, the religious approach that he imbibed was markedly different from other religious men.

He accepts the inner oneness of all existence in the cosmic spirit, and saw all living beings as representatives of the eternal divine reality. Divine presence envelops the whole world and it makes its reflective presence felt in men and women. Gandhiji believed that man's ultimate goal in life was self-realisation. Self-realisation, according to him, meant seeing God face to face, i.e., realising the absolute Truth or, what one may say, knowing oneself. He believed that it could not be achieved unless man identified himself with the whole of mankind. This necessarily involved participation in politics. Politics is the means, par excellence, to engage with the world. Such an engagement is expressed in service. Gandhiji was clear in his mind that Truth could not be attained by merely retiring to the Himalayas or being bogged down with rituals but in actively engaging with the world, keeping oneself open to the voice of God and critically reflecting upon oneself and letting others to reflect on you.

It is only through the means of self-purification that self-realisation can be attained. The fasts, prayers and works of service that he undertook were all directed towards such an end. In his Autobiography, Gandhiji says that self-realisation required self-purification as its ethical foundation. Man's moral life flows from such a search inward into his own self and expresses itself in outward activity of fellowship and concern to others.

Gandhiji invoked the five-fold moral principles: truth, non-violence, non-stealing, non-possession and celibacy. The observance of these moral principles would purify man and enable him to strive after self-realisation.

VIEWS ON HUMAN NATURE

Gandhiji's views on man, human nature and society are in consonance with his philosophical outlook and reflect his convictions regarding morality and ethical pursuit of life. At the same time he was deeply aware of the imperfections of human beings. Conscious as Gandhiji was about man's weaknesses as an individual or a member of a group, he still did not think of man merely or only as a brute. Man, he was convinced, was after all a soul as well. Even the most brutal of men, he felt, cannot disown the spiritual element in them, i.e., their potentiality for goodness.

Man is inherently predisposed towards his self-realisation. In him, moral qualities and social virtues such as love, cooperation, and tolerance preponderate over violence, selfishness and brutality, and man keeps working for higher life. He writes: "I believe that the sum total of the energy of mankind is not to bring us down but to lift us up and that is the result of the definite, if unconscious, working of the law of nature".

Gandhiji believed that human nature is, in its essence, one and that everyman has the capacity for the highest possible development: "The soul is one in all; its possibility is, therefore, the same for everyone. It is this undoubted universal possibility that distinguishes the human from the rest of God's creation."

RELATIONSHIP BETWEEN RELIGION AND POLITICS

The modern world attempted to mark off religion from the political domain and made religion a purely personal, affair. Religious beliefs and commitments by themselves are not supposed to shape the political realm. Against such a position Gandhiji called for the reinsertion of religion in shaping public life and saw an intimate relationship between the health of a polity and religious pursuits.

➢ **Concept of Religion**

According to him, as many religions as there were minds. Each mind, he would say, had a different conception of God from that of the other. All the same they pursue the same God. He insisted that religion be differentiated from ethics. Fundamental ethical precepts are commonn across religions although religions may differ from each other with respect to their beliefs and practices.

Religion enables us to pursue truth and righteousness. Sometimes he distinguished religion in general and religion in a specific sense. One belongs to a specific religion with its beliefs and practices. As one proceeds through the path suggested by it one also outgrows its limitations and comes to appreciate the common thread that binds all religions and pursuers of truth. He said, "Religion does not mean sectarianism. It means a belief in ordered moral government of the universe. It is not less real because it is unseen. This religion transcends Hinduism, Islam, Christianity, etc. It does not supersede them. It harmonises them and gives them reality".

➤ Concept of Politics

Politics, for Gandhiji, was but a part of man's life. Though he thought that an increase in the power of the state did the greatest harm to mankind by destroying individuality which lay at the root of all progress, yet he viewed political power as a means that enabled people to better their conditions in every department of life. Politics therefore is an enabling activity. He wrote, "my work of social reform was in no way less or subordinate to political work. The fact is that when I saw that to a certain extent my social work would be impossible without the help of political work, I took to the latter and only to the extent that it helped the former".

Political activity of man is closely associated with other activities of man and all these activities, according to Gandhiji, influence each other. "Life is one indivisible whole, and all my activities run into one another". Therefore political activity is intimately related to other walks of life and pursuits. What he hated in politics was the concentration of power and the use of violence associated with political power.

➤ Relationship between Religion and Politics   IGNOU Book Q.4

Gandhiji formulated the relationship between politics and religion as an intimate one. Religion cannot be divorced from politics. Given the fundamental objective of life as self-realisation, if politics does not enable religious pursuits it is not worthwhile at all. Politics is intimately related to the entire activities of human life. This is particularly true in modem times. He wrote, "The whole gamut of man's activities today constitutes an indivisible whole. You cannot divide social, economic, political and purely religious work into watertight compartments."

As evident, Gandhiji looked at politics with a view to reform it. He firmly believed that he could lead a truly religious life only when he took part in politics. But the motivation that imbues one in participation in public life is important. The Gandhian view of politics was a politics where people participated in public affairs for purposes of serving others. Hence, for him, all political activities concerned themselves with the welfare of everyone.

For Gandhiji, politics, is one method of seeking a part of the whole truth. Political activity helps man to achieve the capacity to rule himself, a capacity wherein he obeys rules of the society without any external force or external imposition. Religion and politics, so understood, make, a good case for swaraj. He regards concentration of power as detrimental to the individual freedom and initiative.

Gandhiji never considered political power as an end; it was a means to enable people to better their condition in every walk of life. For him political power was a means to regulate public life at varipus levels in tune with the principles stated above. If the life of a polity becomes self-regulated, there was no need to have representative government.

UNITY OF ENDS AND MEANS

That the ends and means are related to each other is one of the basic tenets of Gandhian philosophy. Gandhiji drew no distinction between the means and the ends implying thereby that one leads to the other and that the latter is the effect of the former, Such an assertion, for him, approximates the scientific principle of the relationship between cause and cffect, Gandhiji would not like to attain the noblest end if that was to be achieved through impure means.

> **Relationship between Means and Ends**   **IGNOU Book Q.5**

Gandhi felt that the relationship between means and ends are integral and constitutive. "Means and ends are convertible terms in my philosophy of life". Refucing those who opined that 'means are after all means', he said, "means are after all everything". As the means so the end. There is no wall of separation between means and ends. While good ends have to be cherished they are not in our control. But means are in our control. "Indeed the Creator has given us control (and that too very limited) over means, none over the end. Realisation of the goal is in exact proportion to that of the means. This is a proposition that admits of no exception." Therefore, "If one takes care of the means, the end will take care of itself."

He rebuked those who think that if one seeks good ends the morality of means can be left to themselves. He argued that means and ends are enmeshed into each other. Inspired by the Gita, the ethical principle that he upheld was atmasakti. One does not perform his duty expecting the fruit of his action and does it for the sake of duty. It sought detachment from the fruits of action.

His approach to action was to be stated by him in categorical terms "I have……concerned myself principally with the conservation of the means and their progressive use. I know if we can take care of them, attainment of the goal is assured. I feel too that our progress towards the goal will be in 'exact proportion to the purity of our means. This method may appear to be long, perhaps too long, but I atn convinced that it is the shortest."

SATYA, SATYAGRAHA AND AHIMSA   IGNOU Book Q.6

Truth or Satya, for Gandhiji, is God himself. He therefore changed the statement, "God is Truth", later in his life into, "Truth is God" and suggested that it was one of the fundamental discoveries of his life's experiments. According to Gandhiji, truth is what the inner self experiences at any point of time; it is an answer to one's conscience; it is what responds to one's moral self. He was convinced that knowledge alone" leads a person to the truth while ignorance takes one away from the truth.

Satyagraha means urge for Satya, or truth. Satyagraha is not merely the insistence on truth; it is, in fact, holding on to truth through ways which are moral and non-violent; it is not the imposition of one's will over others, but it is appealing to the reasoning of the opponent; it is not coercion but is persuasion. For Gandhiji, a Satyagrahi is always truthful, morally imbued, non-violent and a person without any malice; he is one who is devoted to the service of all.

Truth, he firmly believed, can be attained only through non-violence which was not negative, meaning absence of violence, but was positively defined by him as love. Gandhiji talked of non-violence of different people. There is the non-violence of the brave: one has the force but he does not use it as a principle; there is the non-violence of the weak: one does not have faith in non-violence, but he uses it for attaining his objectives; there is the nonviolence of the coward: it is not non-violence, but impotency, more harmful than violence. For Gandhiji, violence was a better option than cowardice.

Through non-violence one appeals to the truth that nestles in people and makes the latter realise it in themselves, come around, and join hands in the common march to truth along with those whom they earlier considered as their adversaries. Given the enmeshing of means and ends, Gandhiji, often saw Love, Truth, God and Non-violence as interchangeable terms. Truth or God or Self-realisation being man's ultimate goal in life, this goal can be attained only through non-violence or ahimsa.

CONCEPT OF SWARAJ

Gandhiji's concept of Swaraj was not merely confined to freeing India from the British yoke. Such freedom he desired but he said that he did not want to exchange 'king log for king stork'. Swaraj is not transfer of political power to the Indians. Nor does it mean, as he emphasised, mere political self-determination. For him, there was no Swaraj in Europe; for him the movement of Swaraj involved primarily the process of releasing oneself from all the bondages one is prey to both internal and external. It involves a movement of self-purification too. It is not the replacement of one type of authority by another.

Swaraj is usually translated in English as 'Independence'. Gandhiji, however, gave this term a much deeper meaning. 'The word Swaraj is a sacred word, a Vedic word, meaning self-rule and self-restraint and not freedom from all restraint which 'independence' often means". He saw swaraj as freedom for all plus self-control by all. Gandhi perceived non-violence as the key to attain such freedom and self-control. Non-violence needs to be imbued in our thought, words and deeds. Once non-violence as Love takes possession of these dimensions of the person then a sense of duty prevails over those of rights.

Swaraj is thus a basic need of all. It recognises no race, religion, or community. Swaraj, implying government based on the consent of the people is not a gift which comes from above, but it is something that comes from within. Democracy, therefore, is not the exercise of the voting power, holding public office, criticising government; nor does it mean equality, liberty or security, though important as they all are in a democratic polity. His Swaraj had economic, social, political and international connotations.

ON PARLIAMENTARY DEMOCRACY   IGNOU Book Q.8

Gandhiji did not subscribe to the view that democracy meant the rule of the majority. He gave several definitions of democracy on several occassions. Democracy is a reflective and deliberate activity marking the process of everyone. Democracy extends consideration to the viewpoints of others as it expects consideration to one's own viewpoint. "The golden rule of conduct (in a democracy), he said, "is mutual toleration, seeing that we will never all think alike and that we shall always see Truth in fragments and from different angles of vision. Conscience is not the same thing for all. Whilst, therefore, it is a good guide for individual conduct, imposition of that conduct upon all will be an insufferable interference with everybody-else's freedom of conscience."

Gandhiji was wedded to adult suffrage. He felt that it is the only way to safeguard the interests of all: the minorities, the poor, the dalits, the peasants and women. He hoped that the voters give weight to the qualifications of the candidates, not their caste, community, or party affiliation. He wanted men of character to enter legislatures for even if they commit mistakes they would never do anything against the interests of the voters. Men and women without character elected by the people would destroy the democratic system. Referring to parliamentary democracy in 1931, Gandhi envisaged a constitution of independent India "which will release India from all thraldom and patronage, and give her, if need be, the right to sin".

GRAM SWARAJ OR DEVELOPMENT FROM BELOW
IGNOU Book Q.9

According to the Gandhian thinking, democracy can function smoothly and according to the concept of swaraj only if it is decentralised. "Centralisation as a system is inconsistent with non-violent structure of society". He wanted the centre of power to move from cities to villages. While conceptualising the decentralised system of rule, Gandhi advanced his theory of Oceanic Circle, which he explained in the following words: "In this structure composed of innumerable villages, there will be ever-widening never ascending circles. Life will not be a pyramid with the apex sustained by the bottom. But it will be an oceanic circle whose centre will be the individual always ready to perish for the village, the latter ready to perish for the circle of villages, till at last the whole becomes a life composed of individuals, never aggressive in their arrogance but ever humble, sharing the majesty of,the oceanic circle of which they are integral units."

Therefore, the outermost circumference will not wield power to crush the inner circle but will give strength to all within and derive its own strength from it.

The building blocks of democracy have to be villages. Gandhiji wanted each village to have an annually elected Panchayat to manage the affairs of the village. Each village following the oceanic circle theory would be autonomous yet interdependent. As Gandhiji argued, "My idea of village swaraj is that it is a complete republic, independent of its neighbours for its own vital wants, and yet inter-dependent for many others in which dependence is a necessity".

IDEAS ON THE ECONOMY
IGNOU Book Q.2

Gandhiji's political philosophical ideas came to shape his ideas on the economy centrally. His economic thought revolves around the following normative ideas:

(i) Economic process must work towards equality and non-exploitation

(ii) it must be consistent with fill employment

(iii) it must provide low priced consumer goods which satisfy the needs of the people

(iv) all those industries with sophisticated technology must be in the public sector

(v) no mass production without equal distribution.

For Gandhiji, the two cardinal principles in his economic thought are the promotion of equality together with social justice. For the purpose the three principles which he prescribed are:

(a) of non-possession i.e, economic policies to be pursued on need-base and not on the wantbase

(b) inequality arises with irrational desires to have more than what one wants

(c) in technologically advanced countries, people do not consume goods in the same proportion they produce; labour-intense technologies are to be preferred to the capital-intensive ones.

SARV0DAVA: THE RISE OF ALL

Gandhiji was critical of the path both capitalist and socialist economies had taken, America harbours massive poverty amidst abundant wealth. "America is the most industrialised country in the world, and yet it has not banished poverty and degradation. That is because it neglects the universal manpower and concentrates power in the hands of the few who amass fortunes at the expense of the many." Socialist economies, he felt, put the cart before the horse: "As I look at Russia where the apotheosis of industrialisation has been reached, the life there does not appeal to me.

Against capitalism and socialism, Gandhi proposed the concept of Sarvodaya, which was based on *three basic principles*:

I. that the good of the individual is contained in the good of all;

II. that the lawyer's work has the same value as the barber's, in as much as all have the same right of earning their livelihood from their work;

III. that a life of labour, i.e., the life of the tiller of the soil and the handicraftsman is the life worth living.

THEORY OF TRUSTEESHIP

One of the most original contributions of Gandhiji in the area of economics is the concept of trusteeship. Gandhiji wanted complete equality in so far as the basic needs of the people were concerned. To ensure that those who were rich did not use their property for selfish purposes or to control others, he derived the term "Trusteeship".

He wished that the idea of trusteeship becomes a gift from India to the world. Then there would be no exploitation and no reserve. In these distinctions he found the seeds of war and conflict. He elaborated on his idea of trusteeship extensively. He suggested "as to the successor, the trustee in office would have the right to nominate his successor subject to the legal sanction."

The idea underlying the concept of trusteeship was twofold:

1. All humans are born equal and hence have a right to equal opportunity. This means that all must have their basic needs fully satisfied.

2. All humans, however, are not endowed with equal intellectual and physical capacity. Some would have greater capacity to produce than others. Such persons must treat themselves as trustees of the produce beyond their basic needs.

3. Violence and force as modes of distribution of produce have to be rejected.

EVILS OF INDUSTRIALISM

Gandhiji was against industrialisation on a mass scale because it leads to many insoluble problems such as the exploitation of the villagers, urbanisation, eavironmental pollution etc. He wanted manufacturing to be done in villages and by the villages. This would keep the majority of the people of India fully employed; they would be able to meet their basic needs and would remain self-reliant. Even modern machines could be used provided they did not lead to unemployment and become the rneans of exploitation.

Gandhiji considered the prevailing industrialisation as a disease. 'Let Us not be deceived by catchwords and phrases', he admonished. Modern machines 'are in no way indispensable for the permanent welfare of the human race.' He was not against machinery as such; he was against industrialism, i.e. industrial and mechanical mentality. "Industrialisation is, I am afraid, going to be curse for mankind. Exploitation of one nation by another cannot go on for all time. Industrialism depends entirely on your capacity to exploit......... India, when it begins to exploit other nations - as it must if it becomes industrialised - will be a curse for other nations, a menace for the world".

It is because of this perspective that Gandhi suggested the boycott of mill made cloth and manufacture of handmade cloth in each and every household particularly in the rural areas. The efforts he made to promote Khadi were just a beginning of the movement he wanted to launch to promote village industries in general. One must see Gandhiji's concept of basic education (nai taleem) in relation to his movement for village industries.

CONCEPT OF SWADESHI

Swaraj as we would see later does not mean just political freedom. Gandhi ascribed a far deeper meaning to this term. It means self-control to begin with. Swaraj and Swadeshi go together. Swadeshi is 'that spirit in us which restricts us to use the services of our immediate surroundings to the exclusion of the more remote". Swadeshi will not merely reinforce autonomous local units but also build cooperative relations with others with whom they need to associate.

Swadeshi and self-sufficiency go together. The former is possible only if the latter is accepted as a matter of principle. Each individual, each family, each village and each region would be economically self-reliant. There are two other concepts, which go together with Swadeshi: they are Decentralisation and Cooperation.

The concept of Swadeshi, for Gandhi, is encompassing. In religion, it means to be faithful to our ancestral religion; in politics, it means the use of indigenous institutions; in economics, it emphasised on the use of things produced in the immediate neighbourhood; one must prefer locally produced things even if they are of relatively inferior quality or costly. It does not mean that one should hate foreign-made products. Gandhiji had a place for foreign-made goods, especially medicines and life-saving drugs if they are not produced in the country.

10.2: IGNOU Book Exercise – Solved

1. Explain briefly the philosophical foundations of Gandhiji's political philosophy.
Answer by India Ebook: Read the 1 Shot Concept Above.

2. List the special features of Gandhian economics.
Answer by India Ebook: Read the 1 Shot Concept Above.

3. Highlight the Gandhian concepts of economic equality and swadeshi.

Answer by India Ebook: Gandhiji's economics stressed on equality, social justice, full employment and harmonious labour-capital relations. The last two centuries produced a good number of social thinkers and scientists. Mam offered an alternative to the capitalistic system articulated by Adam Smith. He called it communism. In between capitalism and communism stood socialism.

Capitalism gave rise to colonialism and exploitation of the poor against which Gandhi fought all through his life. But he opposed capitalism as much as communism. For him the individual, his freedom, dignity and satisfying life were more important than mere economic progress, which both capitalism and communism promised to deliver, Anything that did not liberate the man was unacceptable to Gandhi.

Morality and ethics occupy a central place in Gandhian concept of economics. In Gandhian economics, the supreme consideration is the human being. Every man has the right to live and, therefore, to find work to meet his basic needs of food, clothing, shelter, education, health and self-esteem. He felt, 'these should be freely available to all as God's air and water are ought to be. They should not be made a vehicle of traffic for exploitation of others. Their monopolisation by any country, nation or group of persons would be unjust".

Gandhiji argued that we must utilise all human labour before we entertain the idea of employing mechanical power. "Real planning", according to him, "consists in the best utilisation of the whole man-power of India and the distribution of the raw products of India in her numerous villages instead of sending them outside and re-buying finished articles at fabulous prices."

4. Discuss Gandhiji's views on religion and its relationship with politics.
Answer by India Ebook: Read the 1 Shot Concept Above.

5. Comment on Gandhi's views on the End-Means unity.
Answer by India Ebook: Read the 1 Shot Concept Above.

6. Discuss Gandhiji's views on truth and non-violence.
Answer by India Ebook: Read the 1 Shot Concept Above.

8. Discuss Gandhiji's ideas of parliamentary democracy.
Answer by India Ebook: Read the 1 Shot Concept Above.

9. Do the present day village panclrayats meet the requirements of Gram Swaraj?

Answer by India Ebook: Read the 1 Shot Concept Above.

10.3: IGNOU Past 6 Attempts Question – Solved

Dec 2021: Write an essay on Gandhi's views on Swaraj, Sarvodaya and Swadeshi.

June 2019: Examine M.K. Gandhi's views on Swaraj, Sarvodaya and Swadeshi.

June 2020: Write an essay on Gandhi's concept of Swaraj.

Answer by India Ebook: Refer 1 Shot Concept Above.

June 2021: Examine M.K. Gandhi's views on the relationship between religion and politics.

Dec 2020: Describe Gandhi's views on the relationship between religion and politics.

Dec 2018: Analyse Mahatma Gandhi's understanding of the relationship between religion and politics.

Answer by India Ebook: Same as Q.4 of Above.

11. JAWAHARLAL NEHRU

Introduction

Nehru's Scientific Temper

> ➢ Science and Religion
> ➢ Scientific Humanism

Nehru's Theory of Culture

Political Ideas of Nehru

> ➢ On Nationalistn
> ➢ On Democracy
> ➢ Individual Freedom and Equality
> ➢ On Parliamentary Democracy

Nehru on Socialism

Nehru's International Outlook

11.1: One Shot Concepts

INTRODUCTION

The contribution of Jawaharlal Nehru is rightly acclaimed as the maker of modern India. Having faith in the Indian people, he sought to build a democratic polity, an economically modernised nation and a country whose role in the community of nations he perceived clearly. He was both a philosopher as well as a practical political leader. He was influenced by the developments of the 19th and 20th centuries as he found them in the world, but at no point of time, he closed his eyes from the ground realities of the country he belonged. Though he belonged to life of comforts and luxuries, he remained a man of masses.

Jawaharlal Nehru (henceforth, Nehru) was born in 1889. he received education at his home in Allahabad and at Harron and Cambridge. During his seven years stay in England, he, imbibed the traditions of British humanist liberation, subscribing largely to ethos propagated by Mill, Gladstone and Morley. Among those whose ideas influenced Nehru were George Bernard Shaw and Bertrand Russell. He was not a political philosopher like Hobbes, Rousseau, or Marx, but he was certainly a man of ideas as also of action.

Nehru was one of the indomitable fighters of Indian freedom who led the Congress movement alongwith a host of ,other leaders such as Vallabhai Patel, Subhash Chandra Bose, Jaya Prakash Narayan, Rajendra Prasad, to mention a few. He led the interim government in 1946 and became the first Prime Minister of the independent India and occupied this position till his death in 1964. During the period of national movement, Nehru suffered imprisonment many a times and had presided over the Congress a couple of times. He was the Congress President in 1929 when it adopted the historic resolution of 'Purna Swaraj'.

Nehru authored Glimpses of World History, Autobiography and The Discovery of India.

NEHRU'S SCIENTIFIC TEMPER

Nehru was basically a scientist in his approach. In fact, he was the first amongst the nationalist leaders who did recognise the importance of science and technology for the modernisation of the Indian society. For a modern educated Indian and this is true as well, Nehru represented the desire to be modern and scientific in one's outlook. To Nehru, Science constituted the very essence of life, without which, he would say, the modern world would have found it difficult to survive. Science, being the dominant factor in modern life, Nehru asserts, must guide the social system and economic structure.

Like his father, Nehru was an agnostic. Nehru had never been able to absorb the religious devoutness of his mother. In spite of his over thirty years contact with Gandhiji whose prophetic personality impressed everyone, Nehru continued and in fact, remained agnostic. He was not a dogmatic or militant atheist, but he was not a spiritualist either.

➤ Science and Religion

Nehru's scientific temper did not permit him to be dogmatic. He had, therefore, no attraction for any religion, for 11e say nothing more than superstitution and dogmatism in the religion, in any religion. Behind every religion, Nehru arelied, lay a method of approach which was wholly unscientific. But he did recognise that religion does provide some kind of a satisfaction to the inner needs of human nature and give a set of moral and ethical values of life in general. Religion was acceptable to Nehru only to that limited extent. He was not a religious man, nor would he ever spend time, as a routine, for morning and evening worshipping. Science was much preferable to religion, Nehru used to argue and continued.

Secularism is basically the separation of religion from politics. Politics is associated with public activities. Religion is an individual affair, giving everyone the right to practise one's own religion. As a part of religious colnlnullity anyone can share any belief. People observe their religious festivals, rituals and customs. But at the same time, if anybody wants to come out of this belief system, he has a right to do so. If somebody is an atheist, he is free not to have any faith. State is not going to interfere in somebody's belief system.

➤ Scientific Humanism

It is not easy to declare Nehru irreligious; he was, in fact, not opposed to religion. He did recognise that religion 'supplied a cleepor craving of human beings'. According to Nehru, it was from 'faith' that 'the inner imaginative urges' which distinguished man from other begins, flowed, and it was to these urges that the ends of a life bore reference. Science too, Nehru says, suggested the existence of the inner world of spirit, but the latter was beyond the reach of science, for his understanding of science was that it explained the 'How's of the existence but left the 'why's' of its alone'. Obviously then, man had to turn inwards to his intuition to see the world of spirit. Thus, between science and intuition, the role was clear: science could help refine one's senses; intuition could help understand the spiritual world.

Nehru's scientific humanism had the combination of scientific dimension as well as the spiritual dimension. Unlike Gandhi's uni-dimensional approach, there is a in-dimensional approach in Nehru. Nehru himself admitted that it was in the interest of matt to have faith in the essential spirituality of manhood, but he emphasised that faith was merely the concluding end of the rationalist process.

NEHRU'S THEORY OF CULTURE	IGNOU Book Q.2

Nehru could never entertain such a perspective of India's structural cultural continuity, but he did appreciate the vicissitudes of India's historical transformations from the days of the ancient Harappan civilisation to the contemporary one. He was not the man who would acknowledge the revelation of God or Dharma in the Indian cultural manifestations. Nehru is a naturalist determinist wlto upholds physical, geological, zoological, chemical and anthropological data, but sees no spiritual governance of the cosmic process. So with Nehru's historiology, there are no providential dispensation and no emotional attachment to any specific culture.

Though Nehru was a Brahmin, he did not attach any meaning to ritualism; he did admire the Gita gospel of dedicated disinterested altruism, and was never thrilled by the exalted orations of the Visvarupa of the Gita's eleventh chapter. He was more influcnced by Russell and Lenin than by the notion of Nirvana. The external materialistic attempts of the Western-Soviet worlds fascinated Nehru more than the Puranic cosmography of the oriental world. That does not mean that Nehru was all Marxist-Leninist. He did know the strength of Marxism - Leninism, but he also knew that it was weak in domains relating to humanist values, when it ignored the positive aspects of capitalistic system, and also when it came to dwell solely on materialistic factors. Nehru was a blend of the two extremes: the external civilisational advancement together with a quest for die realisation of values in all spheres of human activities.

Nehru's concept of culture was not spiritual, but material; it was not eternal, but humanist; it was, more or less, this worldly, historical and to that extent a blend of secular and temporal, social and economic values. His culture was not dogmatic, fundamentalist, fanatical, narrow, prophetic, angological, divine and godly. It was one that was an apostle of compassion, altruism, humanism and one which was more close to liberty, equality, fraternity, human rights, and rationalistic.

POLITICAL IDEAS OF NEHRU   IGNOU Book Q.3

➤ On Nationalism

Nehru was a great nationalist, though he had no theory of nationalism. He was, indeed, inspired by the concept of cultural pluralism and synthesis. To him, nationalism was a noble phase of self-magnification. By nature, Nehru was a nationalist and was a rebel against authoritarianism and always found himself akin to Bal Gangadhar Tilak.

Nehru's nationalism had its clear distinctive features. It was a composite and a living force and as such could make the strongest appeal to the spirit of man. Only such a type of socialism could be a driving force for freedom, and it alone could give a certain degree of unity, vigour and vitality to many people all over the world. But Nehru did not appreciate the narrow and fanatical type of nationalism. In fact, Nehru's nationalism was a firm commitment to the idea of complete independence of the country. And in 1928, he presided over the Lahore Congress session and got the Purna Swaraj resolution passed.

➤ On Democracy

Nehru was a great champion of democracy, Throughout his life, he laid emphasis on the importance of democracy and desired passionately that independent India would go along the full democratic process. He had a great passion for freedom. Grown in the Western democratic traditions, Nehru absorbed, since childhood, many of the dominant concepts of modern democratic thought. Nehru was a true democrat, for he never doubted the soundness of democracy as a spiritual proposition. Nehru's concept of democracy had specific implications. In the early years of liberation struggle, democracy, for Nehru, meant the ideal of self-rule or responsible government.

➤ Individual Freedom and Equality

Nehru was a democrat by nature, temperament and conviction; he held individual freedom and equality as important components of any democratic polity. According to Nehru, the creative spirit of man could grow only in an atmosphere of freedom. To promote and preserve the values of human life, both society and individual must enjoy freedom. The purpose of a democratic society, Nehru held, was essentially to provide necessary conditions of creative development.

➤ On Parliamentary Democracy

Indian cultural traditions and historical experience under the British rule helped Nehru to support the parliamentary democracy instead of Presidential system of the USA. Parliamentary democracy is much more flexible to accommodate diverse social groups. No social group is allowed to go out of the system as the system is ready to bear the agitation orgaizised by such a group to a point. Even Nehru did not agree to the demands of such groups but accommodated their demands in a democratic process.

NEHRU ON SOCIALISM	IGNOU Book Q.4

Nehru's interest in socialism can be traced to his Cambridge days when the Fabianism of George Bernard Shaw and the Webbs attracted him.The fast changing political, social and economic ideas taking place throughout the world sharpened his socialistic influences. India's millions living in poverty made Nehru a socialist, notwithstanding the Marxist ideology of Marx and Lenin which had its profound impact on him. Nehru was of the opinion that no ideology other than socialism could fit in the democratic pattern as that of India. He was convinced that no democracy could succeed without imbibing socialist pattern.

He laughed off Gandhi's claim to being a socialist and rejected the Marxian thesis of the dictatorship of proletariat. Under India's peculiar conditions, Nehru came to advocate the socialistic, if not socialism, pattern of society. Nehru's concept of socialism was not the abolition of private property, but the replacement of the present profit system by the higher ideal of cooperative service. His socialistn was not the state ownership of the means of production, but was their societal and cooperative ownership. Nehru brought socialism close to democracy.

Nehru's socialism has the distinctive characteristic of progressive industrialisation through which alone the Indian economic problems (poverty, backwardness, low rate of production) could be solved and through which alone the modern India could be built. He strongly believed that in industrialisation. For industrialisation, Nehru ruled out the capitalistic model and pleaded the socialist model by limiting the same to nationalisation of certain key industries and cooperative approach in agriculture while allowing the private sector to participate in industry and agriculture. That was what one may say the essence of socialistic pattern of society......the model which was made to work through

(i) econornic planning;   (ii) mixed economy;   (iii) five years plans.

Nehru's concept of socialism had a vision of future India and of modernising India. He wrote: "For we have to build India on a scientific foundation to develop her industries, to change that feudal character of her land system and bring her agriculture in time with modern methods to develop the social services which she lacks so utterly today."

NEHRU'S INTERNATIONAL OUTLOOK   **IGNOU Book Q.5**

Nehru's significant contribution lies in the evolution and growth of an international outlook. Indeed, he was a great nationalist and as such had a vision of independent India's foreign policy which was in tune with

India's national interest. Non-alignment as foreign policy was nationalistic in its objectives. India could not have devoted itself to modernisation, nor would it have successfully protected her frontiers, had it aligned with any one of the two military blocs. Her economy, politics, social existence, internal circumstances would have been at risk if India would have chosen the path of joining any bloc of the post-war (1945) days. So, if Nehru sought to build an independent non-aligned foreign policy for India, it made sense and brought to the fore Nehru as a nationalist.

But Nehru was, despite his being a nationalist, a great internationalist. He was the architect of non-alignment as a movement and as a force on the international forum. At heart, Nehru was internationalist, an advocate for the United Nations, a champion of the world. He had a role for India in the community of nations.

He used to insist that the states should maintain a reasonable balance between natiollalism and internationalism. Narrow nationalism, according to him, leads to imperialism which he discarded outrightly, to fascism which he denounced at the first opportunity, to exploitation of one state by another which he thought posed a threat to world peace. He would rather visualise the emergence of a world federation, and a world republic, and not an empire for exploitation.

In an age of nuclear fission, hydrogen fusion and the prospects of neutron bombs and chemical warfares, Nehru could have been an apostle of world peace, a champion of disarmament, and a true believer of the ideals of the United Nations. There is only one alternative to world terrorism, and it is, as Nehru rightly says, world peace.

11.2: IGNOU Book Exercise – Solved

1. Explain Nehru's scientific temper and his concept of scientific humanism.

Answer by India Ebook: Nehru was basically a scientist in his approach. In fact, he was the first amongst the nationalist leaders who did recognise the importance of science and technology for the modernisation of the Indian society. For a modern educated Indian and this is true as well, Nehru represented the desire to be modern and scientific in one's outlook. To Nehru, Science constituted the very essence of life, without which, he would say, the modern world would have found it difficult to survive. Science, being the dominant factor in modern life, Nehru asserts, must guide the social system and economic structure.

Like his father, Nehru was an agnostic. Nehru had never been able to absorb the religious devoutness of his mother. In spite of his over thirty years contact with Gandhiji whose prophetic personality impressed everyone, Nehru continued and in fact, remained agnostic. He was not a dogmatic or militant atheist, but he was not a spiritualist either.

➤ Scientific Humanism

It is not easy to declare Nehru irreligious; he was, in fact, not opposed to religion. He did recognise that religion 'supplied a cleepor craving of human beings'. According to Nehru, it was from 'faith' that 'the inner imaginative urges' which distinguished man from other begins, flowed, and it was to these urges that the ends of a life bore reference. Science too, Nehru says, suggested the existence of the inner world of spirit, but the latter was beyond the reach of science, for his understanding of science was that it explained the 'How's of the existence but left the 'why's' of its alone'. Obviously then, man had to turn inwards to his intuition to see the world of spirit. Thus, between science and intuition, the role was clear: science could help refine one's senses; intuition could help understand the spiritual world.

Nehru's scientific humanism had the combination of scientific dimension as well as the spiritual dimension. Unlike Gandhi's uni-dimensional approach, there is a in-dimensional approach in Nehru. Nehru himself admitted that it was in the interest of matt to have faith in the essential spirituality of manhood, but he emphasised that faith was merely the concluding end of the rationalist process.

2. Evaluate Nehru's theory of culture.

Answer by India Ebook: Read the 1 Shot Concept Above.

3. State briefly the main tenets of Nehru's political ideas.

Answer by India Ebook: Read the 1 Shot Concept Above.

4. State the evolution of Nehru's concept of socialism. What are the characteristics of his theory of socialism?

Answer by India Ebook: Read the 1 Shot Concept Above.

5. Explain briefly Nehru international outlook.

Answer by India Ebook: Read the 1 Shot Concept Above.

11.3: IGNOU Past 6 Attempts Question - Solved

Dec 2021: Examine Jawaharlal Nehru's vision of Socialism.

June 2020: Describe Jawaharlal Nehru's understanding of secularism and socialism.

Answer by India Ebook: Same as Q.4 of Above.

June 2019: Describe Jawaharlal Nehru's understanding of scientific humanism.

Answer by India Ebook: Same as Q.1 of Above.

12. B. R. AMBEDKAR

Introduction
Life Sketch
His Writings
B. R. Ambedkar's Thought and Ideas
  ➢ Ideological Orientation
  ➢ Reason and Rights
  ➢ Religion
  ➢ Caste
  ➢ Untouchability
  ➢ Constitutional Demnocracy
Social Justice and Supportive Polity

12.1: One Shot Concepts

INTRODUCTION

Babasaheb Ambedkar is one of the foremost thinkers of modern India. His thought is centrally concerned with issues of freedom, human equality, democracy and socio-political emancipation. He is a unique thinker of the world who himself suffered much humiliation, poverty and social stigma, right from his childhood, yet he rose to great educational and philosophical heights. He was a revolutionary social reformer who demonstrated great faith in democracy and the moral basis of a society. He was one of the principal critics of India's national movement led by M.K. Gandhi.

He built civic and political institutions in India and criticised ideologies and institutions that degraded and enslaved people. He undertook several major studies on the economy, social structures and institutions, law and constitutionalism, history and religion with methodological rigour and reflexivity. He was the Chairman of the Drafting Committee of the Indian Constitution and defended its key provisions with scholarly precision and sustained arguments without losing sight of the ideals it upheld while, at the same time; holding firmly to the ground. He embraced Buddhism, recasting it to respond to modern and socially emancipatory urges, with hundreds of thousands of his followers and paved the way for its resurgence in Modern India.

LIFE SKETCH

Babasaheb Ambedkar (1891-1956) was born in the untouchable Mahar Caste in Maharashtra on 14 April, 1891. He suffered all kinds of social humiliations in childllood as well as in his subsequent life on account of the stigma of untouchability. In the class room he was not allowed to sit along with the rest of the students. He had to drink water only in his handcup in school, poured by members of the upper castes from above. Learning Sanskrit language was denied to him.

Inspite of all these hurdles, he successfully completed his graduation from Bombay University and went on to do his Masters and Ph.D. from Columbia University in U.S.A. He was influenced by the liberal and radical thought currents in America and Europe, more particularly with the thought that emerged following the French Revolution. Struggles against racial discrimination in America helped his resolve to fight against castebased oppression in India. He came to be deeply concerned with untouchability and caste system that prevailed in India. At the same time, he probed the impact that colonialism had on the economy, politics and social life of India.

After he completed his Ph.D. at Columbia University, he returned to serve the administration of Baroda Maharaja who had sponsored his education in America. But even after such exceptional qualifications, he had to suffer the pangs of untouchability in Baroda administration.

In 1936, Dr Ambedkar founded the Independent Labour Party which contested 17 seats in the elections of 1937 in the Bombay Province and won 15 of them. The World War II and the demand of the Muslim League for Pakistan introduced new and complex issues in the national movement. Dr Ambedkar established a different party, the Scheduled caste federationin 1942.

Ambedkar was elected to the Constituent Assembly from Bengal and in the Assembly, made a plea for a united India with the Congress and the Muslim League working together. He was appointed as the Chairman of the Drafting Committee of the Indian Constitution and became the law minister in the Nehru Cabinet in August 1947.

Ambedkar resigned from the Nehru Cabinet in 1951 and strove to work out an alterative to the lack of social and economic democracy in India and the inability of the Constitutional democracy to effectively function in its absence. Such a search eventually led him to conversion to Buddhism and the proposal for the establishment of the Republican Party of India. He died on 6 December, 1956 mourned by millions.

➢ His Writings

Dr. Ambedkar wrote several books. Unlike his contemporaries, he had done a lot of original research on his texts. Apart from writing the Indian Constitltion as the Chairman of its Drafting Committee and defending it in the marathon debates of the Constittrent Assembly, he wrote several books that reflect systematic thinking. Apart from his doctoral dissertations on The Problem of the Rupee (1923) and The Evolution of

Provincial Finance in British India(1925) he wrote Annihilation of Caste(1936), Thoughts on Pakistan (1940), What Congress and Gandhi have done to the Untouchables (1945), Who were the Sudras? (1946), The Untouchables: who were They and done they became Untouchables? (1948), States and Minorities (1947), Thoughts on linguistic States (1955) and his magnum opus The Buddha and his Dharmma (1957) are the most important. Apart from them he wrote numerous articles, submitted learned memoranda, delivered lectures and commented on the issues in the journals he published.

12.2: IGNOU Book Exercise – Solved

1. Comment on Ambedkar's critique of liberalism.

Answer by India Ebook: Dr Ambedkar thought that liberalism upheld a narrow conception of freedom which tolerated huge accumulation of resources in a few hands and the deprivation and exploitation that it bred. He thought that liberalism is insensitive about social and political institutions which, while upholding formal equality, permitted massive inequalities in the economic, social and cultural arenas. He argued that liberal systems conceal deep inequalities of minorities such as the coliditions of the Blacks in U.S.A. and Jews in Europe.

He further argued that liberalism was often drawn to justify colonial exploitation and the extensive injustices it sustained. Liberal stress on the individual ignored community bonds and the necessity of the latter to sustain a reflective and creative self. Further liberalism ignored the repression and the alienation of the self that exploitative and dominant structures bred. He found that liberalism has an inadequate understanding of state and the measures that state has to necessarily adopt to promote and foster good life. He felt that the principle of equality before law is truly a great advance as compared to the inegalitarian orders that it attempted to supplant but it is not adequate. He advanced stronger notions such as equality of consideration, equality of respect and equality of dignity. He was sensitive to the notion of respect and the notion of community was central in his consideration.

2. What were Ambedkar's significant differences with Marx?

Answer by India Ebook: Ambedkar identified certain crucial areas on which he was in tune with Marxism. He argued that the task of philosophy is to transform the world, as Marx suggested in his theses on Feurbach, and he saw the central message of the Buddha as demanding the same. There is conflict between classes and class-struggle is writ large in social relations. He argued that a good society demands extensive public ownership of the means of production and equal opportunity to everyone to develop his or her self to the fullest extent.

He, however, rejected the inevitability of socialism without the intervention of human agency concretely working towards it; the economic interpretation of history which does not acknowledge the crucial role that political and ideological institutions play and the conception of the withering away of the state. He decried the strategy of violence as a means to seize power and called for resolute mass action to bring about-a good society. He underscored the transformative effect of struggles in transforming those launching the struggles and the social relationsm against which they are launched. He further argued that a desirable political order can be created only by acknowledging a moral domain which he saw eminently expressed in the Buddha's teachings.

3. Highlight the characteristics of Brahmanism as an ideology.

Answer by India Ebook: Dr. Ambedkar was very critical of the Brahmanical ideology which, he felt, has been the dominant ideological expression in India. He argued that it reconstituted itself with all its vehemence by defeating the revolution set in motion by the Buddha. It subscribed to the principle of graded inequality in organising social institutions and relations; defended the principle of birth over the principle of worth; undermined reason and upheld rituals and priest-craft. It reduced the shudra and the untouchable to perpetual drudgery and ignominy. It defended inequality and unequal distribution of resources and positions and sanctified such measures by appeal to doctrines such as karma-siddhanta. It upheld the principle of the superiority of mental labour over manual labour. It had little sympathy towards the degraded and the marginalised. It left millions of people in their degraded condition, away from civilisatioa, and defended their abominable conditions. It had little place for freedom and for re-evaluation of choices. It parcellised society into umpteen closed groups making them unable to close ranks, foster a spirit of community and strive towards shared endeavours. It took away from associated life its joys and sorrows, emasculated struggles and strivings and deplored sensuousness and festivity. He constructed Brahmanism as totally lacking in any moral values and considerations based on such values.

4. Identify four issues of conflict between Gandhi and Ambedkar.

Answer by India Ebook: Ambedkar was a bitter critic of Gandhi and Gandhism. He rejected many central notions as propounded by Gandhi such as Swaraj, non-violence, decentralisation, Khadi, trusteeship and vegetarianism. He subscribed to a modern polity with modern economy. This-worldly concerns were central to his agenda rather than other-worldly search. He felt that an uncritical approach to Panchayat Raj will reinforce the dominant classes in tlie countryside handing over additional resources and legitimacy to them to exploit the social classes and groups below them.

He attacked Gandhi's approach to the abolition of untouchability, an approach that denied its sanction in the shastras and which called upon caste Hindus to voluntarily renounce it and make reparations for the same. He saw Gandhi not merely caving in to Hindu orthodoxy but reformulating such orthodoxy afresh, Gandhi was dispensing moral platitudes to untouchables and trying to buy them with kindness while letting others to promote their interests, without hindrance. He rejected the appellation 'Harijan' that Gandhi had bestowed on untouchables alld poured scorn an' it.

5. Discuss the significance of reason in Ambedkar's thought.

Answer by India Ebook: Dr. Ambedkar saw the modern era as heralding a triumph of human reason from myths, customs and religious superstitions. The world and man, he argued, can be explained by human reason and endeavour. The supernatural powers need not be invoked for the purpose. In fact the a supernatural powers themselves reflect weak human capacities and an underdeveloped state of human development: He therefore saw the expression of human Peason manifest in science and modern technology positively. If there are problems with regard to them then the same reason is capable of offering the necessary correctives. Further, he saw knowledge as eminently practical rather than speculative and esoteric. He felt that speculative knowledge divorced from active engagement with practice leads to priest-craft and speculation.

Ambedkar's attitude to religion remained ambivalent. While he did not subscribe to a belief in a personal God or revelation, he felt that religion, as morality, provides an enduring foundation to societies and enables collective pursuit of good life. Such a religion elevates motives, upholds altruism and concern for others, binding people in solidarity and concern. It cares and supports and strives against exploitation, injustice and wrong-doing.

6. Highlight the conception of rights in Ambedkar's thought.

Answer by India Ebook: Dr. Ambedkar argued that freedom, equality and fraternity are essential conditions for good life and a regime of discrete rights need to be constructed on them as the foundation. He understood rights not merely within the narrow confines of liberal individualism but as individual and group-rights. He defenced both types of rights in the Constituent Assembly debates.

Further, he argued for both civil and political right and social and economic rights. He did not see them in opposition but as reinforcing one a other. If there is a conflict between them, they have to be negotiated through civic and political forums. He also subscribed to the rights of minorities and cultural groups to maintain their distinctive beliefs and identities while at the same time affording them proper conditions to take their rightful place in public affairs. He defended preferential treatment accorded to disadvantaged communities not only for reasons of equality but also on grounds of egalitarian social structures, and for the pursuit of a sane and good society.

7. Review Ambedkar's understanding of Hinduism.

Answer by India Ebook: Ambedkar dwelt extensively on major religions of the world, particularly Hinduism, Islam, Christianity and Buddhism. He wrote a great deal on Hindism and Buddhism. The mainstream trajectory of religious evolution that he traced in early India was the Vedic society getting degenerated into Aryan society; the rise of

Buddhism and the social and moral transformation that it brought about and the counter-revolutionn manifest in the development of a specific ideological and political expsession which he termed Brahmanism.

He found that the Hindu scriptures do not lend tbemselves to a unified and coherent understanding. They reflect strong cleavages within and across sects and tendencics. There are cleavages within the Vedic literature; the Upanishadic thought, often, cannot be reconciled with the Vedic thought; the Smriti literature is, quite often, in contention with the Sruti literature; gods come to be pitted against one another and Tantra is in contention with the smriti literature. The avatars of Hinduism, such as Ratna and Krishna, cannot be held up for adulation as exemplaries. He saw the Bhagavadgita as primarily putting forward a set of arguments to save Brahmanism in the wake of the rise of Buddhism and the inabilily of the former to defend itself by appeals to rituals and religious practices.

8. Why does Ambedkar regard Buddhism as appropriate to the modern world?

Answer by India Ebook: Babasaheb Ambedkar is one of the foremost thinkers of modern India. His thought is centrally concerned with issues of freedom, human equality, democracy and socio-political emancipation. He is a unique thinker of the world who himself suffered much humiliation, poverty and social stigma, right from his childhood, yet he rose to great educational and philosophical heights. He was a revolutionary social reformer who demonstrated great faith in democracy and the moral basis of a society. He was one of the principal critics of India's national movement led by M.K. Gandhi.

He embraced **Buddhism**, recasting it to respond to modern and socially emancipatory urges, with hundreds of thousands of his followers and paved the way for its resurgence in Modern India.

Ambedkar developed a new interpretation of Buddhism and saw it as socially engaged. It privileged the poor and the exploited and was concerned with the sufferings and joys of this world. It does not subscribe to the existence of God or the eternity of soul. It upholds reason, affirms the existence of this world, subscribes to a moral order and is in tune with science. He saw the great values of freedom, equality and community as central to the teachings of the Buddha.

9. What do you think of Ambedkar's critique of Christianity and Islam?

Answer by India Ebook: Dr. Ambedkar's thought has inany dimensions. There were very few issues that he left untouched. He formulated his opinion on many crucial questions that India was confronting during his times. His versatility is reflected in his social and political though't, economic ideas, law and constitutionalism.

Ambedkar had both theological and sociological **criticism against _Christianity and Islam_**. Both of them subscribe to a transcendental domain which, apart from its affront to hurnan reason, beget authoritative and paternalistic tendencies. In a sense they dwarf human reason, freedom of enquiry and equality of persons. Their pronouncements cannot be reconciled with scientific reason. Christian belief that Jesus is the son of God militates against reason. Both these religions, he felt, accommodated themselves to graded inequality and ranking to different degrees. Their precepts have often led their adherents to resort to force and violence. He saw the Buddha standing tall against the protagonists of both these religions.

10. Highlight the characteristic features of untouchability, according to Ambedkar.

Answer by India Ebook: Ambedkar distinguished the institution of untouchability from that of caste although the former too is stamped by the same principle of graded inequality as the fatter. Untouchability is not merely an extreme form of caste degradation but a qualitatively different one as the system kept the untouchable outside the fold and made any social interaction with him polluting and deplorable. He argued that in spite of differences and cleavages all untouchables share common disadvantages and meted out the same treatment by caste Hindns: they are condemned to ghettoes on the outskirts of the village, are universally despised and kept away from human association.

He did not subscribe to the position that untouchability has its basis in race. He saw it as a social institution defended by the ideology of Brahmanism. While he did not extensively probe the reasons for the origin of untouchability in one instance, he proposed a very imaginative thesis that untouchables were broken men living on the outskirts of village communities who, due to their refusal to give up Buddhism and beef-eating, came to be condemned as untouchables.

11. Why does Ambedkar think that struggle against untouchability has to be launched on several fronts?

Answer by India Ebook: Given the deep-seated beliefs and practices of untouchability prevailing in India, Ambedkar thought that no easy solution can be found for the malaise. **Removal of untouchability** required the transformation of the entire society wherein respect and rights towards the other person becomes a way of life rather than a mere constitutional mechanism. Given the entrenched interests and prejudices revolving around the institution of untouchability, it was something too much to expect from entrenched groups. Therefore he felt that the primary burden of emancipating themselves fell on the untouchables themselves. Such-self-help required not only struggles but also education and organisation, Further a constitutional democracy with preferences at various levels can help enormously in such an endeavour.

12. Highlight the reasons for Ambedkar's defence of constitutional Democracy.

Answer by India Ebook: The major area of Ambedkar's work was on constitutional democracy. He was adept in different constitutions of the world particularly those that provided an expansive notion of democracy. Rule of law as a bond uniting people and according equal participation of people in collective affairs was quite central to his imagination. He was deeply sensitive to the interface between law on one hand and customs and popular beliefs on the other.

He however felt that customs may defend parochial interests and popular beliefs might be deeply caught in prejudices and may not uphold fairness. They may not be in tune with the demands of time, morality and reason. But if law upholds freedom and democracy then it could be placed at the service of common good. Given the long-drawn prejudices and denial of justice in public culture he thought that the role of the state based on law and democratic mandate is crucial. He envisaged a democracy informed by law and a law characterised by sensitivity to democracy. Law upheld reason and morality but without the authoritative injuhctions of law, the former had no teeth.

Such a stress on democracy and law made Ambedkar to strongly stress the autonomy of the state. State needs to transcend the parochial interests galore in society which often tend to reduce the state as an instrument of their purpose. He argued that ascriptive majorities which are permanent, and not amenable for political dissolution and reconstitution, too can be considered as parochial interests. They can undermine rights but at the same time pretend that they are upholding constitutional democracy.

12.3: IGNOU Past 6 Attempts Question – Solved

Dec 2021: Briefly describe B.R. Ambedkar's views on social and economic democracy.

Dec 2020: Write an essay on Dr. B. R. Ambedkar's views on social and economic democracy.

June 2019: Describe Dr. B.R. Ambedkar's views on social and economic democracy.

Dec 2018: Examine Dr. B.R. Ambedkar's views on social and economic democracy.

Answer by India Ebook: Almost Same as Q.12 of Above.

Introduction
Theory of Freedom and Self-Realisation
Emphasis on Human Reason
Critique of Nationalism
Differences with Gandhi
Analysis of Bolshevism

13.1: One Shot Concepts

INTRODUCTION

Rabindranath Tagore (1861-1941) was an outstanding literary figure of India who exerted considerable influence on human thinking in the contemporary world. This influence extended to the political arena as well by his lucid elucidation of important concepts like nationalism, freedom, human ratiollality and his many differences with Mahatma Gnntlhi's (1869-1948) philosophy and strategies.

While Gandhi was a political and social activist and Tagore was a poet, there was remarkable consistency in the enunciation of their major political themes, which they developed and refined reflecting on major events of their time. Furthermore, in Tagore there was a quest of a poet for human perfection and completeness and not merely a pragmatic analysis of a particular problem or a sitnatian. The modern Indian political tradition of assimilating the Western ideas with the Eastern ones, which began with Rammohan Roy, reached its culmination in Tagore.

THEORY OF FREEDOM & SELF-REALISATION IGNOU Book Q.1

A specific Indian idea of freedom that started to evolve with Rammohan, was articulated subsequently by Swami Vivekananda (1863-1902), Aurobindo Ghosh (1872-1950), Gandhi and Tagore. Rammohan wanted to synthesist Indian and Western ideas with an unflinching commitment to his own tradition. Vivekananda like Rammohan was rooted in the Indian tradition. Aurobindo, Gandhi and Tagore reiterated his emphasis on harmony without losing sight of one's identity and culture.

For Tagore, freedom was not merely political emancipation but the mingling of the individual with the universe depicted in his song- my freedom is in this air, in the sky and in this light of universe. The goal of freedom lay in making one perfect. He significantly remarked that many nations and people were powerful but not free because realisation of freedom was something very different from merely using coercive power.

For Tagore, freedom of the individual was the basis or the growth of human civilisation and progress. It was the inner urge of a person to be in harmony with the great universe. Freedom was everything creative and spontaneous in human mind and spirit. It was the capacity to create a better order. Tagore was against unquestioned conformity which he described as "the state of slavery which is thus brought on is the worst form of cancer to which humanity is subject".

Tagore, like the early Indian liberals considered the real problem of India as social and not political. A narrow vision of political liberty would grossly be inadequate in establishing a good society for that would deny individual's moral and spiritual freedom. He castigated even the free independent countries being a reflection of this narrow view. Mere political freedom could not make one free, as cleavages and weaknesses of society would pose a danger to politics.

EMPHASIS ON HUMAN REASON

In Sabhyatar Sankat or Crisis in Civilisation (1941) he mentioned his admiration of the humanistic tradition of English literature, which formed the basis of his faith in modern civilisation. He admitted that India's link with the outside world was established with the arrival of the British and cited Burke, Macaulay, Shakespeare and Byron as those who inspired and generated a confidence in the triumph of the human being.

Indians aspired for independence but believed in English generosity and the British character, which reflected their philosophy of universal fellowship. Like other contemporary Indian thinkers, Tagore also believed that India benefitted from her contact with the West in general and Britain in particular. He considered the British victory over India as the victory of modernity. The right to freedom in a modern world is a basic human right.

Tagore not only mentioned how as a young person he was immensely influenced by John Bright but also the pain he felt at the denial to Indians the industrial power that made Great Britain a world power. He also pointed out to the lack of modernity and absence of scientific temper in

India, a void filled by coming into contact with the West thereby making the 19th century an age of co-operation with Europe. However Europe in the 20th century failed by its own criterion for it was unable to transmit its basic civilisation traits to others.

CRITIQUE OF NATIONALISM   IGNOU Book Q.2

Tagore's perception of the dual role, one positive, "the spirit of the West" and the other negative, "the nation of the West" was the starting point of his analysis of nationalism as it developed in the West. He paid glowing tributes to the achievements of the West in the field of literature and art which he described as "titanic in its uniting power..., sweeping the height and the depth of the universe" and also mentioned the presence of outstanding individuals fighting for the cause of humanity.

The nation, which represented the organised self-interest of a whole people, was also the "least human and least spiritual" and the biggest evil in the contemporary world. It build a "civilisation of power" which made it exclusive, vain and proud. One form of its manifestation was the colonisation of people and subjecting them to exploitation and suffering. In this context Tagore cite the example of Japan-which had secured the benefits of Western civilisation to the maximum possible extent without getting dominated by the West. He considered the nation to be nothing else than an "organisation of politics and commerce."

Its emphasis on success made it a machine that stifled harmony in social life and eclipsing the end of good life, namely the individual. He mentioned the anarchists who opposed any form of imposition of power over the individual. He rejected the philosophy of a balance of terror on the premise that man's world was a moral one.

DIFFERENCES WITH GANDHI   IGNOU Book Q.3

The essence of Gandhi's entire political philosophy is in the Hind Swaraj (1908) and Tagore's in Swadeshi Sanzaj (1904). Both of them had a great deal of respect and reverence for one another. A major controversy erupted between them following Gandhi's return to India from South Africa and his meteoric rise in Indian politics culminating in the non co-operation movement and Tagore's articulation of a philosophy of universalism and his criticism of the cult of nationalism during the First World War.

Tagore, regarded India's basic problem to be social and not political, though like Gandhi, he was conscious of the acute differences and conflicts in the Indian society. As such society and not politics was his primary area of focus. Tagore developed this argument after a careful scrutiny of the Gandhian leadership and strategy. He derived the basic framework of this evaluation from his earlier experiences during the days of agitation against Bengal partition of 1905. In that movement, initially Tagore took an, active part popularising Raksha Bandhan and nationalistic songs.

Tagore's first written evidence about Gandhi's preferences and policies were in a letter written on 12th April 1919 from Shantiniketan advising Gandhi to be cautious about the programme of non co-operation for in no way did it represent India's moral superiority. He took note of the important changes that came with the rise of Gandhi in Indian in Indian politics. He thought very highly of Gandhi's leadership and could also see that the proposed non-cooperation movement would engulf the whole country and would be much bigger than the anti-partition movement of Bengal. Disagreeing with Gandhi, Tagore pointed out that it was not possible to estimate the exact magnitude of the middle class and that peasants who constituted 80% of the Indian population without a meaningful occupation for six months in'a year.

ANALYSIS OF BOLSHEVISM IGNOU Book Q.4

Tagore visited Europe and the United States several times but he went to the USSR only once when he was 70 years old and considered the trip a pilgrimage and felt that had he not gone his life would have remained incomplete. The trip was for two weeks only and he could not go anywhere else except to be in Moscow. The Letters from Russia expressed his recollections of the Soviet Union.

Tagore appreciated the fact that the Bolsheviks had ended many of the evil practices of the Czarist regime except one important practice, that of suppression of opinion and advised the Bolsheviks to end this evil. He was always against unquestioned allegiance, which was one of his criticisms of Gandhi's leadership in India. He, as a believer in the importance of freedom of mind, could easily see the dangers of suppression of dissidence and alternative points of view within the Soviet system. He was against the preaching of anger and class hatred, which the Soviets taught and that any good society must acknowledge the existence of difference of opinion through freedom of expression.

13.2: IGNOU Book Exercise – Solved

1. Discuss Rabindranath Tagore's idea of freedom atid self-realisation.
Answer by India Ebook: Read the 1 Shot Concept Above.

2. Explain Tagore's critique of nationalism.
Answer by India Ebook: Read the 1 Shot Concept Above.

3. Discuss and distinguish the basic disagreement between Tagore and Gandhi.
Answer by India Ebook: Read the 1 Shot Concept Above.

4. Evaluate Tagore's views on Bolshevism.
Answer by India Ebook: Read the 1 Shot Concept Above.

13.3: IGNOU Past 6 Attempts Question – Solved

Dec 2021: Discuss Tagore's ideas on nationalism.
Dec 2018: Critically examine Rabindranath Tagore's critique of Nationalism.
Answer by India Ebook: Almost Same as Q.2 of Above.

June 2021: Examine Rabindranath Tagore's vision of freedom.
Dec 2020: Critically analyse Rabindranath Tagore's vision of nationalism and freedom.
Answer by India Ebook: Almost Same as Q.1 of Above.

14. COMMUNIST THOUGHT: M N ROY AND E M S NAMBOODIRIPAD

Introduction

Evolution of Communist Movement in India

The Establishment of Communist Party

The Communist Party of India before Independence

The Communist Party of India after Independence

- Towards Parliamentary Strategy
- Towards Divisions from Within
- Towards Cooperation of the Communist Farces

M N Roy: From Marxism to Radical Humanism

- Roy's Marxism
- Humanist Critique of Marxism
- Roy's Radical Humanism

E M S Namboodiripad: The Conimunist Theoretician

- Marxist-Leninist Theory
- On Caste Conflicts
- National Unity
- Strategy of Indian Revolution
- Indian History

14.1: One Shot Concepts

INTRODUCTION

Communist thought in India has its origins in the writings of Karl Marx, Friedrich Engels and their followers. The Bolshevik Revolution of October 1917 had a tremendous impact on the entire world. The social democratic parties, reflecting the thoughts of Marx and Engels, had already been established in the major countries in Europe. The Bolshevik revolution in Russia created the erstwhile Soviet Union and the communist parties came to be established in various parts of the world, especially in Asia, Africa and the Latin American countries for strengthening the on-going liberation struggles and providing a boost to the spread of communist thought.

The Indian Communist Party was established in 1924 and worked in close association with Communist movements guided and inspired by the Communist International also called the Comintern. M N Roy, with his characteristic Marxian views, influenced the world communist movement, though he was disillusioned by commmunism in later life. The Indian Communist Leader and Theoretician EMS Namboodiripad kept holding the red flag till the end of his life. Communist thought in India is an interesting account of the development of the Marxian thought and philosophy as it grew in the Indian conditions.

EVOLUTION OF COMMUNIST MOVEMENT IN INDIA   IGNOU Book Q.1

Like all the Marxist, the Indian communists together with the other communists, believe in the destruction of capitalism and the eventual establishment of a socialist/communist society. The Indian Communists regard imperialism as the highest stage of capitalism, just the way Lenin did. In India, the communists believe and in fact, propagate that the working class in alliance with the other toiling masses is alone capable of bringing about the socialist revolution. They also believe in proletarian intenationalism.

The communist movement in India, thus, has its intellectual and ideological roots in the philosophy of Marxism. The Indian Marxists not only accept Marxism, but also interpret the Indian socio-political developments in the Marxian style; at times, the interpretation seems imposed while at others, it becomes a victim of over-simplification. They accept the following Marxist formulations as gospels beyond any doubt:

b The state and society are distinct entities: the type of society dictates the type of state. Accordingly, the state is not independent of society; its relationship with society is that of a superstructure and a base.

ii) The state is an instrument of the society: those who control the society also control the state; the state is the state of the dominant class.

iii) The state, in a class society, is also a class institution and as such seeks to establish the values of society. The capitalist state is the state of the capitalists, by them and for them.

iv) In a capitalist society, the working class will organise itself and will seek to overthrow the capitalist society; in the pre-capitalist society, the workers along with the capitalists could overthrow the feudal society.

v) With the abolition of the capitalist class society, there would usher the classless socialist society, which with its political organ - the dictatorship of the proletariat - would establish socialism and pave way for a classless - stateless communist society.

THE ESTABLISHMENT OF COMMUNIST PARTY

The Communist Party of India was founded in September, 1924 possibly at the initiative of Satya Bhakta of Uttar Pradesh. There were only 78 members belonging to the Indian Communist Party at the time or its foundation. Later the membership rose to 250. Some differences emerged within the Communist Party in relation to its link with the Communist International. Although the Communist Party of India was not legally a component of the Communist International, its ties with the international revolutionary movement were nevertheless being consolidated. There were closer links with the Communist Party of Great Britain. Its delegation of George Allison and Philip Spratt came to India in 1926-27.

The communists, must before the formation of the legal Communist Party of India, had associated themselves with the liberation struggle. The Kanpur Conspiracy Case in 1924, was decided against the communist leaders - SA Dange, Nalini Gupta, Mauzaffar Ahmed and Shaukat Usmani - awarding them imprisonment.

The Communist Party of India, by 1928-29 had set before itself the goal of creating a mass-scale revolutionary organisation and an anti-imperialist alliance. The sixth world Congress of the Communist International, in September 1928, had passed a resolution to strengthen the communist parties and the trade union organistions in the colonial countries and warned such bodies against the national-reformist bourgeois organistions, including the temporary agreements with them over agitations launched against imperialistic forces.

THE COMMUNIST PARTY OF INDIA BEFORE INDEPENDENCE   Q.6

Years after its formation, the Communist Party of India sought to strenghthen its position in the trade unions, organising them, guiding them and propagating Marxism and Leninism so as to prepare them for revolutionary struggle against the nationalist bourgeoisie and the imperialistic- capitalistic forces in the sphere of trade union movement, the Communist Party of India (CPI) did achieve definite success by making inroads in the workers' bodies.

In the 1930's, the CPI adopted a United Front from above by aligning itself with the nationalist movement, but it kept its separate identity among the workers and the peasants. The CPI, as it was a banned organisation, came closer to the Congress and numerous communists joined the Indian National Congress (INC) and formed socialist group within the congress, which came to be known as the Congress Socialist Party (CSP).

With the axis power Germany invading the Soviet Union in 1941 during World War II, and with the Soviet Union joining the Allied powers, the situation of the Indian Communists became precarious. The ban on the CPI by the Britishess in India was lifted and the CPI which was until then, considering the 1939 war bourgeois war, began not only suffering the war, but also declared it as the people's war against the fascists. The CPI did not support the 1942's Quit India Movement.

The communists were divided over the question of independence of the country which was only a couple of months away, especially after the formation of the interim government headed by Jawaharlal Nehru.

THE COMMUNIST PARTY OF INDIA AFTER INDEPENDENCE   Q.6

(i) Towards Parliamentary Strategy

With relatively a more militant left, the CPI immediately after independence, adopted a United Front tractic from below: aligning itself with the workers and peasants against the Indian National Congress. Now, the CPI strategy was on course of a revolution - with strikes, sabotage and violence. CPI was officially advised to abandon 'adventurous' tactics and to adopt the policy of contesting Parliamentary Elections.

(ii) Towards Divisions From Within: The dismissal of the Kerala Communist Government in 1959 made the CPI's relations with the Congress strained. The Chinese invasion of India in 1962 made polarisation rather evident in the CPI beyond any repair. CPI attributed the split to the Chinese machination. The CPI(M), though neutral on the ideology issue, came to be dubbed as hostile to the Soviet position.

(iii) Towards Co-operation of the Communist Forces: Ideologically, the two communist parties remained apart; the CPI aligning with nationalist-bourgeois forces while the CPI(M) working its own strategy of people's democratic government. With the CPI on the decline, especially after the disintegration of the Soviet Union as a single state, the two communist parties are drawing close to each other, and, now coming up with a United Front election manifesto.

14.2: IGNOU Book Exercise – Solved

1. Mention, in brief, the growth of communist movement in India.
Answer by India Ebook: Read the 1 Shot Concept Above.

2. Distinguish between Socialism and Communism.
Answer by India Ebook:

3. How far was M N Roy influenced by Marxism? On what grounds did he differ from Marxism?
Answer by India Ebook: MN Roy began his political life as a militant nationalist, believing in the cult of the bomb and the pistol and the necessity of armed insurrection. The futility of this path made him a socialist and then a communist. He joined the Communist International, but was thrown out of it as he differed from its aim of being a movement all over the world. Roy passed through *three phases* in his career.

In the first phase, which lasted up to 1919, he was a national revolutionary, struggling arms for the terrorists of Bengal.

In the second phase, Roy was a Marxist engaged in active communist movement first in Mexico and then in Russia, China and India.

In the last and final phase, Roy emerged as a radical humanist, completing his journey from Nationalism to Communism and from Communism to Radical Humanism.

He was in his student life, a revolutionary as well as an intellectual. He had a zest for new ideas and a quest for freedom. This is how he drifted from Marxism towards Radicalism. Marxism and Radicalism constitute the characteristics of his philosophy.

According to Roy, **Marx's theory of class struggle** has subordinated individual consciousness. He was also critical of Marx giving too much prominence to the working class. To him, polarisation of capitalist society into the exploiting and the working class never takes place. The middle class does not disappear. It is the middle class which produces revolutionaries. Lenin recognised this fact, but failed to recognise the middle class as a class. Thus, Roy denounced the theory of class struggle.

Roy did not regard surplus value as a peculiar feature of capitalism. The creation of surplus value and the accumulation of capital were also necessary in a socialist society. The only difference between a socialist society, unlike capitalist society, was that the surplus value was not appropriated by a particular class.

Roy made very serious observations about India's polity. He remarked that the Indian traditions of leadership lend themselves to authoritarianism. Leader is considered infallible. The presence of a charismatic leadership indicates the fascist tendency in the Indian politics. One may agree with Roy that India lacks a democractic tradition and the existence of peculiar social structure and the tendency to hero worship makes for authoritarian tradition. His warning about the Facist danger in the politics has proved to be true.

4. What were Roy's Ideas on Radical Humanism?

Answer by India Ebook: In the later years of his life, Roy became an exponent of "New Humanism". He distinguished this from other humanist philosophy and termed it radical. Though Roy is influenced in his approach by the scientific materialism of Hobbes, Ethics of Spinoza and Secular politics as propounded by Locke, he reconciled all these to propound a rational idea of freedom with the concept of necessity. The central purpose of Roy's Radical Humanism is to co-ordinate the philosophy of nature with social philosophy and ethics in a monistic system. "It is for this reason that Roy claims it as humanist as well as materialist, naturalist as well as nationalist, creativist as well as determinist".

i) Roy's idea revolves around Man. As a radical Humanist, his philosophical approach is individualistic. The individual should not be subordinated either to a nation or to a class.

ii) Roy presents a communal pattern of social growth. Groups of human beings settled down in particular localities for the cultivation and the organisation of society.

iii) Roy was a supporter of not only a democracy where every citizen will be informed and consulted about affairs of the state, but also of radical democracy as well. The basic feature of radical democracy is that the people must have the ways and means to exercise sovereign power effectively.

iv) Roy also contemplated an economic reorganisation of the society in which there would be no exploitation of man by man. It would be a planned society which would maximise individual freedom. This is possible when society is established on the basis of cooperation and decentralisation.

v) Education would important in Radical democracy. As a radical humanist, Roy came to believe that a revolution should be brought about not through class struggle or armed violence, but through education.

vi) Roy emphasised the concept of moral man. To him politics cannot be divorced from ethics. Roy traces morality to rationality in man. Reason is the only sanction for morality. Without moral men, there can be no moral society.

5. Mention the contribution of EMS Namboodiripad to the communist thought in India.

Answer by India Ebook: Ernakulam Manakkal Sankaran Namboodiripad (1909-1998) was one of the architects of United Kerala, a renowned, brave and committed socialist, historian and Marxian theoretician wook took an active part in the communist movement of India. During his college days, he was associated with the Indian National Congress and the struggle for freedom. In 1934 he joined the Congress Socialist Party and was later elected as the Kerala State Congress Secretary.

E.M.S Namboodiripad belonged to the more militant wing of the Communist Party. Me was deeply disturbed by the fiercely anti-Chinese foreign policy the congress had adopted after the Sino-Indian border war in 1962 and by the Congress role in overthrowing the C.P.I led government in Kerala in 1959.

Naniboodiripad said that the destruction of the 'age-old' village system and the development of the new capitalism by the British administration resulted in two apparently contradictory features in the Indian society and politics: the emergence of working class as a class and the disruption of the unity of the working class and the toiling people as evidenced in the increasing conflicts between 'backward' and 'forward castes'. These tensions were built into the national movement in which the leaders often highlighted the revival of the 'age-old' Indian civilisation and culture thereby emphasising division of society into a hierarchical system of castes.

Namboodiripad was of the opinion that although historians claim to be 'impartial', 'objective' and interested only in 'discovering the truth', their work invariably reflects the philosophy of the class they belong to. Some of the historians stand for particular religious communities, regional, linguistic or cultural groups or communities. Their writings often reflect their approaches to the problems of the history and culture of India. The political philosophy of EMS Namboodiripad is indeed a valuable contribution to the growth of social sciences of the contemporary society.

6. Trace the Indian Communist thought before and after independence.

Answer by India Ebook: Read the 1 Shot Concept Above.

14.3: IGNOU Past 6 Attempts Question – Solved

June 2021: Analyse M.N. Roy's views on Radical Humanism.

Answer by India Ebook: Same as Q.4 of Above.

Dec 2020: What do you understand by M. N. Roy's model of partyless democracy?

Answer by India Ebook: Almost Same as Q.3 of Above.

15. SOCIALIST THOUGHT: RAMMANOHAR LOHIA AND JAYAPRAKASH NARAYAN

Introduction
History of Socialist Movement in India
Congress Socialist Party: Programmes and Policies
Socialist Thought of Dr. Rammanohar Lohia
Socialist Thought of Jayaprakash Narayan

14.1: One Shot Concepts

INTRODUCTION

The growth of socialist thought as a philosophy af social and economic reconstruction is mostly the product of the Western impact on India. One of the leading saint-philosopher of India, Aurobindo Ghosh's criticism of the middle class mentality of the leaders of the Indian National Congress and his plea for the social development of the "proletariats" in his asticles to the magazine "Indu Prakash in 1893, B. G. Tilak's reference to the Russian Nihilists in the Kesari in 1908, C.R.Das's reference to the glorious role of the Russian Revolution in the contemporary international system, and particularly his emphasis on the role of the trade union movements in the structural development of the social and political system of India, in his Presidential address at the Gaya Session of the Indian National Congress in 1917, and Pandit Jawaharal Nehru's eloquence about the New Economic Policy of 1926 and other developments in the Soviet Union in his articles and books such as Soviet Russia, Autobiography and Glimpses of World History, are some of the examples of the impact of the Soviet ideas and thoughts on the minds of the leading Indian thinkers and political leaders.

HISTORY OF SOCIALIST MOVEMENT IN INDIA   IGNOU Book Q.1

The socialist movement became popular in India only after the First World War and the Russian Revolution. The unprecedented economic crisis of the twenties coupled with the capitalist and imperialist policies of the British Government created spiralling inflation and increasing unemployment among the masses.

A number of radical groups and youth leagues opposing the policies of the British government were born in India. A left wing was created within the Congress Party under the leadership of Jawaharlal Nehru and Subhas Chandra Bose. In Novemver 1928 an organistion called the Independence for India League was created under the leadership of S. Srinivas Iyengar. Both Nehru & SC Bose were its joint secretaries. This left oriented pressure group within the Congress spearheaded the movement for complete political, social and economic independence.

In the Lahore Session of the Congress, in 1929, Jawaharlal Nehru, with the help of this left wing group, got a resolution for complete independence passed. After this resolution for independence was passed, the Independence for India League got slowly disintegrated. During the first two decades of the 20th century a number of political parties based on religion, caste, and community came into existence in India.

As a result of the impact of the Russian Revolution, most of the left parties were formed in the Third World countries. The Communist Party of India (CPI) was born in 1925. This left party was linked with the Communist International of Moscow. Besides, a lot of radical splinter groups also were born in different parts of India.

CONGRESS SOCIALIST PARTY: PROGRAMMES & POLICIES

IGNOU Book Q.2

The birth of the Congress Socialist Party in May 1934 was a landmark in the history of the socialist movement of India. While assessing the programmes and policies of the Congress Socialist Party, it will be desirable to remember the contribution of the Meerut Conspiracy case in spreading the ideology of the early 1930s. Besides, the creation of the All India Kisan Sabha in 1936, and the role of the Youth League and Independence for India League can never be ignored in the growth of the socialist thought in India. The Congress Socialist Party provided an all Indian platform to all the socialist groups in India.

The ideology of the Congress Socialist Party was a combination of the principles of Marxism, the ideas of democratic socialism of the British Labour Party, and socialism mixed with the Gandhian principles of Satyagraha and non-violence. The Party was under the influence of deep Marxist ideas in its formative phase. The leading members of the Congress Socialist Party belonged to different streams of thought.

Some of the leaders of the Congress Socialist Party (CSP) like AN Deva and Jayprakash Narayan were the strong supporters of the Marxist trend in the CSP.

The socialists played an important role in the 1942 Quit India Movement, and in organised trade union movements of the country. Their increasing popularity was neither lilted by the leading members of the Congress nor by the communists and the Royalists. The Congress leaders were not very sympathetic to the role of the socialists inside the Congress organisation.

During the socialist movements in the pre independence phase, and subsequently during the 1940s, 50's and 6O's, greater emphasis was put on the acceleration of agricultural production, cooperative, land ceiling, reduction of unemployment, and the raising of the living standards of the suppressed and backward communities.

SOCIALIST THOUGHT OF DR. RAMMANOHAR LOHIA   IGNOU Book Q.3

Rammanohar Lohia articulated his approach in what he called Seven Revolutions such as equality between man and woman, struggle against political, economic and spiritual inequality based on skin colour, removal of inequality between backward and high castes based on traditions and special opportunity for the backward, majors against foreign enslavement in different forms, economic equality, planned production and removal of capitalism, against unjust encroachments on private life, non proliferation of weapons and reliance on Satyagraha were the basic elements of his thought. In his book on Marx, Gandhi and Socialism, Lohia made an alanysis of principles of democratic socialism as an appropriate philosophy for the successful operation of constructive programmes.

Lohia made a significant contribution in the field of socialist thought in India. He always laid greater emphasis on the combination of the Gandhian ideals with the socialist thought. He was a proponent of the cyclical theory of history. He believed that through the principles of democratic socialism the economy of a developing country could be improved. Although Dr. Lohia was a supporter of dialectical materialism he put greater emphasis on consciousness. He was of the opinion that through an internal oscillation between class and caste, historical dynamism of a country could be insured. According to Dr. Lohia, the classes represent the social mobilisation process and the castes are symbols conservative forces.

Lohia was very popular for his Four Pillar State concept. He considered village, mandal (district), province and central, government as the four pillars of the state. He was in favour of villages having police and welfare functions. He propounded his theory of New Socialism at Hyderabad in 1959. This theory had six basic elements. Lohia was opposed to doctrinaire approach to social, political, economic and ideological issues. He wanted the state power to be controlled, guided, and framed by people's power and believed in the ideology of democratic socialism and non-violent methodology as instruments of governance. Lohia was convinced that the concept of "welfare-statism" was not an answer for the social and economic progress of countries in the Third World.

As a socialist thinker and activist, Lohia has carved out for himself a unique place in the history of Indian socialist thought and movement. Although there has been a tendency among the contemporary researchers not to recognise him as an academic system-builder in the tradition of Kant, Hegel or Comte, his democratic socialist approach to look at ideology as an integrated phenomenon is now being widely accepted throughout the world.

SOCIALIST THOUGHT OF JAYAPRAKASH NARAYAN   IGNOU Book Q.4

Jayaprakash Narayan popularly known as JP was a confirmed Marxist in 1929. By the middle of 1940s he was inclined towards the Gandhian ideology. Till 1952 JP had no faith in non-violence as an instrument of social transformation process. The transformations of the Russian society in the late 1920s had thereafter changed his outlook towards Marxism and the process of dialectical materialism. Soviet Union was no more an ideal model for him for a socialist society.

JP was convinced that there was inter-relationship between nature of the revolution and its future impact. He was convinced that any pattern of violent revolution would not lead to the empowerment of people at the grassroots level. JP was very much critical of dialectical materialism on human development. He was convinced that this methodology would affect the spiritual development of man. His concept of Total Revolution is a holistic one. He used this term Total Revolution for the first time in a British magazine called The Time in 1969.

The concept of Total Revolution as enunciated by JP is a confluence of his ideas on seven revolutions i.e. social, economic, political, cultural, ideological and intellectual, educational and spiritual. JP was not very rigid regarding the number of these revolutions. He said the seven revolutions could be grouped as per demands of the social structures in a political system. JP was deeply moved by the mutilation of democratic process, political corruption and fall of moral standards in our public life. He said that if this pattern of administrative process continues then there would not be any socialism, welfarism, government, public order, justice, freedom, national unity and in short no nation.

14.2: IGNOU Book Exercise – Solved

1. Explain the history of socialist movement in India.
Answer by India Ebook: Read the 1 Shot Concept Above.

2. Discuss the evolution and origin, programme and policies of the Congress Socialist Party.
Answer by India Ebook: Read the 1 Shot Concept Above.

3. Examine the Socialist Thought of Dr. Rammanohar Lohia.
Answer by India Ebook: Read the 1 Shot Concept Above.

4. Explain the Socialist Thought of Jayaprakash Narayan.
Answer by India Ebook: Read the 1 Shot Concept Above.

5. Critically evaluate the relevance of the Socialist Thought in the Contemporary Indian Society.
Answer by India Ebook: It is often said that the Indian socialist literature did not attain the depth and theoretical maturity like that of Plekhanov, or Bukharin or Rosa Luxemburg. But one must not forget that the significance of Indian Socialist thought lies in its emphasis on

the needs of original socialist thinking in the context of agrarian, caste bound underdeveloped economy and polity of India. The German Marxists considered the peasants as reactionary elements. The socialist thought in India highlighted the role of peasants in the structural development of the economy.

The Indian Socialists were interested to eliminate the prevailing class and caste struggles of Indian society. They indeed brought about some original thitlking on the basic problems of Indian society - the role of peasants, caste struggle and planning in an under developed economy. They were for the synthesis of political liberty and economic reconstruction with the emphasis on the Gandhian principles of Non Violence and Satyagraha. This indeed is their contribution to the Indian Socialist thought.

14.3: IGNOU Past 6 Attempts Question – Solved

Dec 2021: Examine the Socialist thought of Jayaprakash Narayan.

Dec 2020: Examine the socialist thought of Jai Prakash Narayan.

Dec 2018: Write an essay on the Socialist thought of Jayaprakash Narayan.

Answer by India Ebook: Same as Q.4 of Above.

June 2021: Write an essay on the development of the Socialist Movement in Pre-Independence India.

Answer by India Ebook: Almost Same as Q.1 of Above.

June 2020: Describe the salient features of Dr. Ram Manohar Lohia's Political Thought.

Answer by India Ebook: Same as Q.3 of Above.

June 2019: Describe in brief the history of socialist movement in India.

Answer by India Ebook: Same as Q.1 of Above.

www.ingramcontent.com/pod-product-compliance
Lightning Source LLC
Chambersburg PA
CBHW041330120726

48005CB00014B/2192